W9-CAO-444

CHARTER

OF THE NEW URBANISM

Patrick J. Pinnell

CONGRESS FOR THE NEW URBANISM

This publication was made possible, in part, by a grant from the Fannie Mae Foundation.

Library of Congress
Cataloging-in-Publication Data

The charter of the new urbanism/essays by Randall
Arendt...[et al.] ; edited by Michael Leccese and
Kathleen McCormick.
    p. cm.
"Congress for the New Urbanism."
 Includes index.
 ISBN 0-07-135553-7
 1. Metropolitan areas—United States. 2. Cities and
Towns—United States. 3. Regional planning—
United States. 4. City planning—United States.
5. Neighborhood—United States. 6. Architectural
design. I. Leccese, Michael. II. McCormick, Kathleen.
III. Congress for the New Urbanism.

HT334.U5 C478 1999
307.760973—DC21   99-051560

McGraw-Hill

A Division of The McGraw-Hill Companies

Copyright © 2000 by The McGraw-Hill Companies, Inc.
All rights reserved. Printed in the United States of
America. Except as permitted under the United States
Copyright Act of 1976, no part of this publication may
be reproduced or distributed in any form or by any
means, or stored in a data base or retrieval system, without the prior written permission of the publisher.

1234567890 QKP/QKP 90432109

ISBN 0-07-135553-7

DESIGN:
Wolfe Design, *Pittsburgh, Pennsylvania*

PRINTED AND BOUND BY:
Quebecor/Kingsport

McGraw-Hill books are available at special quantity
discounts to use as premiums and sales promotions,
or for use in corporate training programs.

For more information, please write to the Director
of Special Sales, McGraw-Hill, 11 West 19th Street,
New York, NY 10011. Or contact your local bookstore.

CHARTER

OF THE NEW URBANISM

Foreword by

SHELLEY R. POTICHA

Essays by

RANDALL ARENDT

G. B. ARRINGTON

JONATHAN BARNETT

STEPHANIE BOTHWELL

PETER CALTHORPE

THOMAS J. COMITTA

VICTOR DOVER

ANDRES DUANY

DOUGLAS FARR

RAY GINDROZ

KEN GREENBERG

JACKY GRIMSHAW

DOUGLAS KELBAUGH

WALTER KULASH

BILL LENNERTZ

WILLIAM LIEBERMAN

WENDY MORRIS

ELIZABETH MOULE

JOHN O. NORQUIST

MYRON ORFIELD

ELIZABETH PLATER-ZYBERK

STEFANOS POLYZOIDES

HENRY R. RICHMOND

MARK M. SCHIMMENTI

DANIEL SOLOMON

MARC A. WEISS

ROBERT D. YARO

Commentary by

HARVEY GANTT

TONY HISS

RICHARD E. KILLINGSWORTH

GIANNI LONGO

TOM SCHMID

Afterword by

PETER CALTHORPE

Postscript by

ROBERT DAVIS

Edited by

MICHAEL LECCESE AND KATHLEEN McCORMICK

CONGRESS FOR THE NEW URBANISM

McGRAW-HILL

NEW YORK   SAN FRANCISCO   WASHINGTON, D.C.   AUCKLAND   BOGOTÁ   CARACAS

LISBON   LONDON   MADRID   MEXICO CITY   MILAN   MONTREAL   NEW DELHI   SAN JUAN

SINGAPORE   SYDNEY   TOKYO   TORONTO

CHARTER OF THE NEW URBANISM

Preamble

THE CONGRESS FOR THE NEW URBANISM views disinvestment in central cities, the spread of placeless sprawl, increasing separation by race and income, environmental deterioration, loss of agricultural lands and wilderness, and the erosion of society's built heritage as one interrelated community-building challenge.

We stand for the restoration of existing urban centers and towns within coherent metropolitan regions, the reconfiguration of sprawling suburbs into communities of real neighborhoods and diverse districts, the conservation of natural environments, and the preservation of our built legacy.

We recognize that physical solutions by themselves will not solve social and economic problems, but neither can economic vitality, community stability, and environmental health be sustained without a coherent and supportive physical framework.

We advocate the restructuring of public policy and development practices to support the following principles: neighborhoods should be diverse in use and population; communities should be designed for the pedestrian and transit as well as the car; cities and towns should be shaped by physically defined and universally accessible public spaces and community institutions; urban places should be framed by architecture and landscape design that celebrate local history, climate, ecology, and building practice.

We represent a broad-based citizenry, composed of public and private sector leaders, community activists, and multidisciplinary professionals. We are committed to reestablishing the relationship between the art of building and the making of community, through citizen-based participatory planning and design.

We dedicate ourselves to reclaiming our homes, blocks, streets, parks, neighborhoods, districts, towns, cities, regions, and environment.

Contents

Foreword

What we now recognize as "New Urbanism" began with a remarkable set of conversations aimed at systematically changing the ground rules for development in North America. In October 1993, the first Congress convened in Alexandria, Virginia, to share works in progress and debate issues. Among the 170 people who attended were some of the nation's leading designers, as well as a number of maverick practitioners. What resulted was energizing and created the seed of a larger movement that has now borne fruit.

The original Congress participants were concerned about the placelessness of modern suburbs, the decline of central cities, the growing separation in communities by race and income, the challenges of raising children in an economy that requires two incomes for every family, and the environmental damage brought on by development that requires us to depend on the automobile for all daily activities.

They discussed root causes—changing household demographics, land consumption without regard to natural features or physical limits, federal and state policies that encourage low-density sprawl, street standards that are insensitive to human needs, and zoning codes that virtually require an ugly sameness to permeate all communities regardless of regional climates and traditions. They analyzed the regional forces that create dilapidated urban neighborhoods surrounded by flourishing suburbs. And, unlike many critics who came before them, they focused on the relationships among these problems.

Fortunately, they didn't stop by enumerating the problems. They sought examples (and created new models) that showed another path. By the end of 1993, it was apparent that these issues also were interesting to many others. Six architects at the forefront of this emerging movement— Peter Calthorpe, Andres Duany, Elizabeth Moule, Elizabeth Plater-Zyberk, Stefanos Polyzoides, and Daniel Solomon—took steps to incorporate as a nonprofit organization that would advocate for the principles of New Urbanism and for a wholesale shift in the way communities are built.

The Congress for the New Urbanism (CNU) seeks to support an American movement to restore urban centers, reconfigure sprawling suburbs, conserve environmental assets, and preserve our built legacy. We aim to achieve this by educating other design professionals, policy makers, and the public; by changing policies and practices that perpetuate destructive development practices; and by forming a network of like-minded groups that can effect change at all levels. CNU is one of only a few voices addressing the confluence of community, economics, and environment in our cities. And it is the only national organization dedicated to addressing these issues through urban design and planning.

Many local, regional, and national groups look to CNU for expertise in land development strategies. But what I find so remarkable about CNU is that it is the only group of planners and designers, and now, also, developers, public officials, and activists, clearly committed to addressing the social and economic implications of design decisions. Granted, the New Urbanists are not the first to posit these ideas—others made many of these points years before the term New Urbanism was even coined. Nor do New Urbanists claim to have invented urbanism. Rather, the New Urbanists have formed an organization dedicated to addressing the problems and publicizing the alternatives.

At this writing, CNU is rapidly growing stronger and more diversified. What began as an odd collection of designers, visionaries, and agitators now includes some of the nation's most esteemed academics, economists, planners, transportation engineers, sociologists, and environmentalists. As a progressive core of practitioners in their respective fields, these CNU members work tirelessly to influence their professions. CNU also hosts a growing number of developers who see New Urbanism as a way to right some wrongs in their profession without neglecting their profits. And, perhaps most encouraging, CNU includes among its ranks a growing cadre of elected officials and citizen activists who view New Urbanism as a means of reclaiming their communities.

In its short existence, CNU has made considerable progress in advancing its ambitious agenda. The most dramatic indicators are the growing numbers of New Urbanist development and redevelopment projects under way around the nation. In addition, there are many indications that public discourse about cities and development has recently made a radical shift, as evidenced by New Jersey Governor Christine Todd Whitman's 1998 inaugural address:

"Every part of New Jersey suffers when we plan haphazardly.... Sprawl eats up our open space. It creates traffic jams that boggle the mind and pollute the air. Sprawl can make one feel downright claustrophobic about our future."

Meanwhile, Vice President Al Gore has made sprawl a national issue:

"While the blight of poor development and its social consequences have many names, the solutions, pioneered by local citizens, are starting to coalesce into a movement. In the future, livable communities will be the basis of our competitiveness and economic strength."

For the first time, there is broad—though far from universal—recognition that the problems of our cities and suburbs need to be addressed and that the planning and design of our cities have ramifications in every aspect of public and private life.

This book focuses on the Charter of the New Urbanism. Adopted by our members in 1996, the Charter sets forth a positive vision for our communities. Its preamble demonstrates the New Urbanists' commitment to tackling problems in an interdisciplinary way, and involving those most affected by design decisions: citizens. As you will see in the essays that follow, its principles are detailed but flexible prescriptions for city design.

I don't expect the Charter to be a stagnant document. The ideas and strategies of New Urbanism need to mature and evolve. We need to learn new and better ways of building and rebuilding. However, the Charter is unique because it promotes a vision and tells how we can accomplish it.

Over time, I hope that the work of the New Urbanists will support what I see as an impending cultural shift. In the twilight of the 20th century, people are increasingly concerned about both their quality of life and maintaining a basic standard of living. They are concerned about civic issues and building a civil community. I see New Urbanism as one piece of a movement whose time has come.

SHELLEY R. POTICHA

Executive Director

Congress for the New Urbanism

What's New About the New Urbanism?

JONATHAN BARNETT

Most of us live amid space, comfort, and convenience that once only the very rich could imagine. Computers, automobiles, and air travel have opened up vast new opportunities for jobs and leisure. But the old methods for managing urban growth and change don't work as well as they used to; often they don't work at all.

In fast-growing suburban areas, communities are trying to control immense new developments with zoning and subdivision codes that were probably enacted in the 1950s to shape much smaller projects, and are struggling to finance new schools, roads, and services. Meanwhile, the landscapes and the way of life that attract the new development become more endangered every day.

Older cities are finding that downtown renewal is not enough to offset lost jobs from vanishing industries, the growing need for social services, problems in the school system, and dysfunctional housing projects.

Older suburbs, which were getting along well until a few years ago, are suddenly confronted by the same kinds of social problems found in the nearby city, without the benefit of the city's tax base and institutional resources.

The Charter of the Congress for the New Urbanism begins:
The Congress for the New Urbanism views disinvestment in central cities, the spread of placeless sprawl, increasing separation by race and income, environmental deterioration, loss of agricultural lands and wilderness, and the erosion of society's built heritage as one interrelated community-building challenge.

Each of these issues has long been identified as a problem. What is new about the New Urbanism is the assumption that solutions to these problems require that they be worked out together.

It is harder to create new jobs in the old city when communities on the urban fringe are offering industrial development subsidies as well as cheap land and new infrastructure. Communities in fast-growing suburbs can't afford the new schools they need, while older suburbs are turning unneeded schools into senior-citizen centers. Whole neighborhoods of houses in cities such as Detroit and St. Louis have deteriorated and been demolished, leaving block after block vacant, but complete with all the necessary utilities. Meanwhile farms and woodlands are being bulldozed for new houses in nearby rural counties, which are going deeply into debt to pay for roads and sewage-treatment plants.

Some cities have grown by annexation to include most of the suburban development in their metropolitan region. Studies show that such metropolitan cities, or city–county governments, have better resources for solving their problems than cities and suburbs that remain separate places. The metropolitan region has become the basic unit of urban development: Airports and highways serve a whole region and not just individual cities and towns. So do retail and office centers, sport franchises, and cultural institutions.

Despite the temptations for individual families and businesses to move away from problems in older cities and suburbs to new homes in the country, no nation can afford a strategy of writing off its older urban areas and replacing them with developments on the edge of metropolitan regions. To state such a policy explicitly is enough to show how absurd it is. However, in the United States, many individual decisions are being made as if older cities and towns are write-offs; and the sum of these individual decisions risks becoming a national policy.

The places where people and businesses are moving often do not live up to expectations. They lack the coherence of older cities and towns. They lack the rural charm people thought they were moving to enjoy. Disappointment with new urbanized areas causes people and businesses to move outward once again, and the whole wasteful cycle is repeated.

Of course it is not possible to rewind development back to, say, 1970, and replay it based on what we know now. Decentralized metropolitan regions are the new reality, and we have to learn how to make them work.

However, it is possible to reshape endless commercial strip development into towns and special districts, and to turn shapeless subdivisions into neighborhoods; but the task is unprecedented and will require the invention of new planning policies and design techniques. It is possible to bring new development into the bypassed and deteriorated areas of cities, but what is offered has to be as good or better than what is available elsewhere. It is possible to make sure that the mistakes of recent urban development are not repeated. It is also possible to link all the diverse parts of the metropolitan region together again with transportation systems that do not rely only on automobiles. Success in these areas would take development pressures off the natural environment and bring new life to valuable old buildings and districts.

So here is another aspect of what is new about the New Urbanism: It calls for new design concepts to meet new situations. These include innovative ways to retrieve the mistakes of recent development; new regulations and policies to keep the old mistakes from recurring; visionary proposals for making older areas competitive again; plans for limiting the extent of the metropolitan region and pulling it together by new forms of transportation.

The Charter continues:
We stand for the restoration of existing urban centers and towns within coherent metropolitan regions, the reconfiguration of sprawling suburbs into communities of real neighborhoods and diverse districts, the conservation of natural environments, and the preservation of our built legacy.

All very well, but how practical are new design concepts, given today's harsh economic and social realities? What about crime; what about schools; what about jobs?

The rapid transformation of cities and suburbs into metropolitan urban regions has been part of a larger process of economic growth and change that has destabilized and transformed many aspects of life today, and goes far beyond issues of city design and planning.

However, some recent innovations in crime control have interesting analogies to the kinds of proposals that are part of the New Urbanism: community-based police patrols, low tolerance for "environmental" offenses like aggressive panhandling or graffiti, plus new computer-aided programs for the strategic deployment of police resources. The success of these innovative crime-control measures contains important messages.

First of all, it turns out that rising crime statistics are not inevitable. Crime can be controlled. It is not necessary to try to move away from it. Second, measures based on community responsibility and environmental improvement are not just good city design. They are also good social policy.

The failure of school systems to educate all children to their full abilities is another massive problem, aggravated by the concentration of families with the most severe economic and behavioral difficulties in older urban areas. Enough evidence has accumulated from experimental programs to demonstrate that, while a few children may have severe learning disabilities, the problem is most often the system and not the children.

The United States is in the midst of a national debate about how to improve schools while maintaining universal education, including proposals and experimental programs for national standards, charter schools, and school vouchers. Some of the most promising innovations include means to involve parents in the life of the schools, school-based programs to help parents in areas with large concentrations of multi-problem families, and community-based support networks of tutors and extracurricular activities. Another important factor is the maintenance of an orderly and secure environment within the school itself.

Again these proposals create interesting analogies to principles of the New Urbanism because they emphasize both a supportive community and the importance of the physical environment.

New international patterns of trade, the changing geography of industrial development, and the rising importance of service and information-based jobs have transformed the workplace. Older cities are no longer the automatic source of low-skilled, entry-level jobs, although many people most in need of these jobs still live in older urban areas.

These issues involve the whole economy and go far beyond the subject matter of city design and planning. The United States and other countries are in the process of adjusting social-welfare policies to place more emphasis on returning welfare recipients to the workforce. This requires greater public-policy emphasis on job creation and correcting the mismatch between the location of jobs and the homes of people who need them. These efforts and many other government economic-development programs involve issues of importance to the New Urbanism. Many bypassed or underused sites in older areas lie idle because of real or suspected industrial contamination. Brownfield programs that make it easier to clean up and recycle these properties can bring life back to older areas. Enterprise Zones provide tax subsidies to encourage businesses to locate near

where people need jobs. Fair housing and other programs encourage decentralization of subsidies to locate affordable housing more evenly across the metropolitan area. New metropolitan transportation systems recognize and serve the decentralized work locations created in recent decades.

The New Urbanism has come a long way from the belief that an earlier generation's design and planning policies, such as Slum Clearance, Urban Renewal, or New Towns, could by themselves cure major societal afflictions.

As the Charter continues:
We recognize that physical solutions by themselves will not solve social and economic problems, but neither can economic vitality, community stability, and environmental health be sustained without a coherent and supportive physical framework.

Frequently new commercial buildings or housing developments, even if very expensive, are seen to detract from their surrounding area rather than to improve it. This is true both in "greenfield" situations and in older urban districts. As a result, local citizens often bitterly oppose new development proposals, a major factor in diverting development farther out to the edges of metropolitan areas.

Much of the conflict between local citizens and developers is unnecessary. It results from outmoded development regulations and the ways that development practice has adapted to them.

For example, most ordinances governing the way properties are divided up into lots set a maximum grade for streets, often 5 percent. The easiest way for a developer to deal with this requirement is to regrade the whole property so that no slope is greater than 5 percent by bulldozing all existing vegetation, shaving off topsoil, pushing soil and rock into runoff watercourses, and, in general, violating basic principles of ecological design. The answer to this problem involves revising local regulations to reduce permitted development in steeply sloping areas while accepting a more flexible layout of lots and streets. At the same time, homebuilders need to revise their standard practice, and not follow plans that require extensive regrading. After all, grading costs money. Mature vegetation has monetary value to the home buyer. And a layout that preserves the contours of the landscape can provide just as many house sites as one that does not.

Another example: Communities often create zones of thousands of acres that permit only one size of single-family house. Developers then construct tracts of hundreds, sometimes even thousands, of the same-size house and lot, producing little diversity of income, no local shopping, few destinations within walking distance, and households located too far apart to support public transportation. Communities instead need to create neighborhood zones that permit a diversity of housing types while incorporating convenience shopping districts. They must permit compact development around neighborhood centers so people can walk to some destinations, and take public transit to others. The effect of this change in policy, where it has been tried, has been to create places of character and diversity, not just a group of subdivisions and the occasional shopping mall.

A third example: zoning that encourages commercial development only in narrow strips along a highway. The idea of the commercial strip goes back to streetcar suburbs and small towns with a single Main Street. It makes little sense as a development pattern extended for miles along highways. However, development practice has adapted to it. People forget that, far from being an inevitable consequence of the real-estate market, commercial strips are created by an outmoded zoning practice that designates far too much commercial land to be used intensively, while not zoning enough commercial land at any one location to permit more efficient development. An alternative pattern concentrating development at specific locations along a highway would create better community design, make long-distance traffic move much faster, use land more efficiently, and generally make more economic sense.

Commercial strip and large-lot zoning deployed over vast acreage are the recipe for urban sprawl. To change the design of new development, it is necessary to change these legal templates.

Here then is another innovation of the New Urbanism: the recognition that design and planning concepts cannot be separated from their implementation mechanism. Today's defects in city design can be traced to defective public policies and poorly thought-out investment practices. Hence the improved city-design concepts advocated by the New Urbanism also require improved public policies and new real-estate investment practices.

As the Charter of the New Urbanism states: *We advocate the restructuring of public policy and development practices to support the following principles: neighborhoods should be diverse in use and population; communities should be designed for the pedestrian and transit as well as the car; cities and towns should be shaped by physically defined and universally accessible public spaces and community institutions; urban places should be framed by architecture and landscape design that celebrate local history, climate, ecology, and building practice.*

Historically, concepts about the design of buildings, landscapes, or cities have been put forward by designers who expect society to recognize the "rightness" of the design and then find ways to implement it. The Congress for the New Urbanism recognizes that innovations in city design require parallel innovations in public policy and private finance. The Congress seeks to be much more than a society of design professionals. It includes all those whose voices need to be heard if there are to be constructive changes in the ways cities and towns are developed—and in society's overall relation to the natural and built environment.

Another aspect of what is new about the New Urbanism and the Congress: It is not just another professional organization, but a coalition of designers, other professionals, public and private decision-makers, and concerned citizens.

To quote the Charter once again: *We represent a broad-based citizenry composed of public and private sector leaders, community activists, and multidisciplinary professionals. We are committed to reestablishing the relationship between the art of building and the making of community, through citizen-based participatory planning and design.*

Of course no group has all the answers. Innovation in city design and in urban and landscape conservation requires experiments, and a continuous process of evaluation and improvement. However, there are some basic principles that can be expected to hold true for a long time. Most of these principles are not new at all; unfortunately they have often been forgotten in the rush to keep up with recent growth and change.

This book sets out 27 basic principles of urbanism that should guide public policy, development practice, urban planning, and design. They begin at the scale of the metropolitan region, and of whole cities and towns. These are followed by design principles for neighborhoods, districts, and corridors as the basic elements of cities and towns, and then city-design principles for blocks, streets, and individual buildings. Each principle is explained and illustrated in detail.

Individually most of these principles will not seem radical. Some may appear to be axiomatic. Yet it is an innovation to consider them as a comprehensive sequence dealing with the built environment at every scale. Together these principles form the basic agenda of the New Urbanism.

As the Charter concludes: *We dedicate ourselves to reclaiming our homes, blocks, streets, parks, neighborhoods, districts, towns, cities, regions, and environment.*

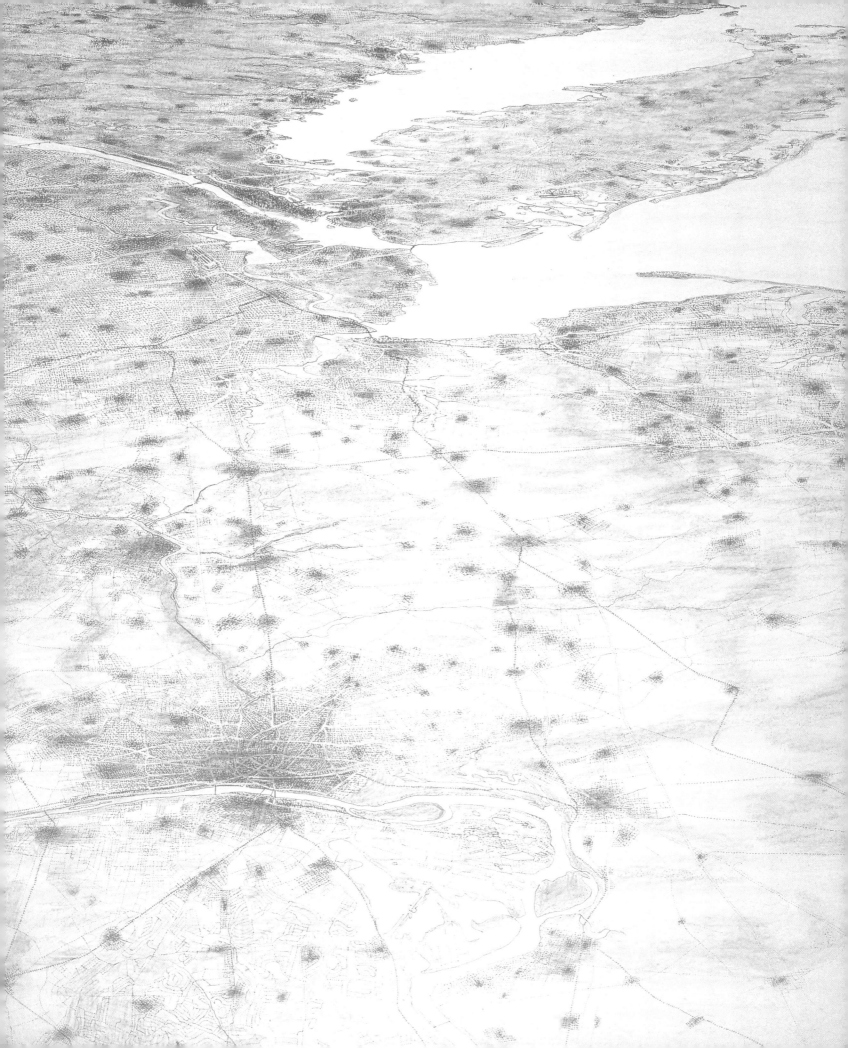

THE REGION: METROPOLIS, CITY, AND TOWN

The largest scale of the Charter is the Region: Metropolis, City, and Town. Many national issues now addressed at the federal, state, and local levels are truly regional in scope. Yet we lack the tools to respond to these challenges at the scale at which they can be resolved. Our aggregations of cities, towns, and suburbs must coalesce into a regional metropolis that is a single economic, cultural, environmental, and civic entity. Given this reality, regional strategies and coordination must guide policies for economic development, pollution control, open-space preservation, housing, and transportation. The Charter outlines emerging strategies of regionalism and their critical design and policy principles.

In opening essays, Peter Calthorpe and Robert Yaro define opportunities for cooperation within metropolitan areas rather than pitting city against suburb. Randall Arendt describes why farmland is still worth fighting for within metropolitan regions. Jacky Grimshaw relates that non-governmental, regional coalitions can advance metropolitan goals. In parallel commentary, Harvey Gantt defines why cities are still vital within New Urbanism. Wendy Morris lays out a program for physical planning that can be achieved on neighborhood and regional scales at the same time. Stephanie Bothwell argues that neighborhoods of the past can provide a prologue for the way we live in the future. Henry Richmond creates an economic case for distributing affordable, transit-oriented housing throughout a region. G. B. Arrington tells us about the Portland region, which has given equal rights and opportunities to pedestrians, cyclists, and transit-riders, and how these concepts have translated into changes in physical design. Finally, Myron Orfield discusses the successes and challenges of a tax revenue–sharing program he helped invent in the Minneapolis–St. Paul region.

One

The metropolitan region is a fundamental economic unit of the contemporary world. Governmental cooperation, public policy, physical planning, and economic strategies must reflect this new reality.

PETER CALTHORPE

The last half-century has seen the rise of a social and commercial geography that fuses town, city, and suburb into a new but unresolved order—the metropolitan region. It's becoming clear that the economic building blocks of the global economy are regions—not nations, states, or cities. It's equally clear that many of our environmental challenges are regional in scope. Air quality, water quality, habitat restoration, and farm-land preservation reach beyond the scale of city and town while remaining unique to each region. Our basic infrastructure investments also are regional in scale and scope. Issues of economic equity, social integration, and race all now play themselves out in a regional geography increasingly segregated by identity, opportunities, and population. And as our cities and suburbs grow together economically, we find ourselves in a new metropolitan culture built out of regional institutions, history, ecologies, and opportunities. Our sense of place is increasingly grounded in the region rather than nation, town, or city.

Yet we have no framework for this new reality, no handle to guide it, nor any established means to harvest its opportunities. Some of our most vexing problems—urban decay and joblessness, sprawl, congestion, lost open space, and economic competitiveness—need solutions that recognize the new economic and social unity of our regions, rather than the piecemeal policies of local governments or bureaucratized

"A great city is nothing
    more than a portrait
    of itself, and yet when
    all is said and done, its
    arsenal of scenes and
    images are part of a
    deeply moving plan."
MARK HELPRIN
Winter's Tale

"This sets the chief mission
    for the city of the future:
    that of creating a visible
    regional and civic structure,
    designed to make man at
    home with his deeper self
    and his larger world...."
LEWIS MUMFORD
The City in History

state and federal programs. Too often we are caught between national solutions that are too generic, bureaucratic, and large, and local solutions that are too isolated, anemic, and reactionary.

Lacking regional tools of governance that employ the opportunities of the new metropolitan reality, policy makers persist in treating the symptoms of our problems rather than addressing their root causes. We address inner-city disinvestment more with localized strategies such as the Community Reinvestment Act legislation, small community banks, tax breaks, and subsidies, rather than by reinforcing such local programs with regional policies that limit sprawl, and with local tax-base sharing to target economic investment where it is needed most. We control air pollution with standards for tailpipe emissions, fuel consumption with more efficient engines, and congestion with more freeways, rather than regionally coordinating transit investments and land-use policy to reduce auto use. We limit lost open space with piecemeal acquisitions, habitat degradation with disconnected reserves, and farmland conversion with convertible tax credits, rather than defining compact and environmentally sound regional forms. Too often, we address affordable housing by building isolated blocks of subsidized housing within low-income neighborhoods, rather than zoning for mixed-income neighborhoods everywhere and implementing regional fair-housing practices.

Effective regional governance can coordinate our patterns of development and renewal in a fashion that goes to the root of these problems, addressing their causes as well as manifestations. It's hard to envision a successful region that does not integrate land-use patterns and transportation investments to create alternatives to increasingly expensive and unsustainable "auto-only" environments. It's hard to envision a healthy regional economy without adequate and well-placed affordable housing for its workforce. It's hard to imagine a high quality of life without access to open space and habitat, and the breathing room provided by preserved farms at the edge of the metropolis. And it's hard to imagine arresting urban decay without some form of regional tax-base equity along with strategies to deconcentrate poverty and improve inner-city schools.

The following five regional strategies involving governmental cooperation, public policy, physical planning, and economic strategies can help reshape the quality of our communities, the health of our environment, and the vitality of our economy. They can help form the framework for more integrated regions and the foundation for many of the principles of New Urbanism at the town, neighborhood, and building scale.

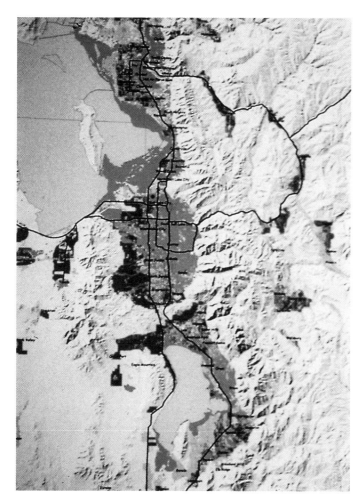 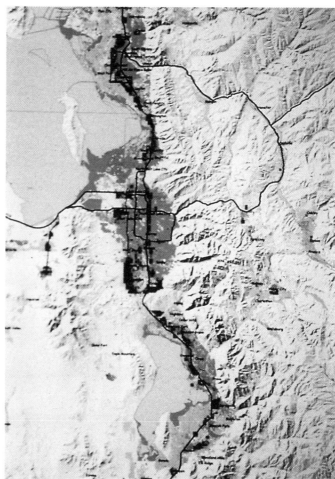

IN 1998, THE SALT LAKE CITY REGION launched the "Envision Utah" plan.
Sponsored by the nonprofit Coalition for Utah's Future, this study examined four
growth scenarios, from almost completely automobile dependent (left) to nearly
90 percent of growth focused in compact, walkable, transit-oriented communities (right).
Citizens learned that auto-oriented growth alone would increase urbanized land by
409 square miles in 20 years. Compact growth would add only 85 square miles. Based
on a survey of citizen preferences (600,000 questionnaires were mailed), Envision
Utah hopes to limit newly urbanized land to 125 square miles.

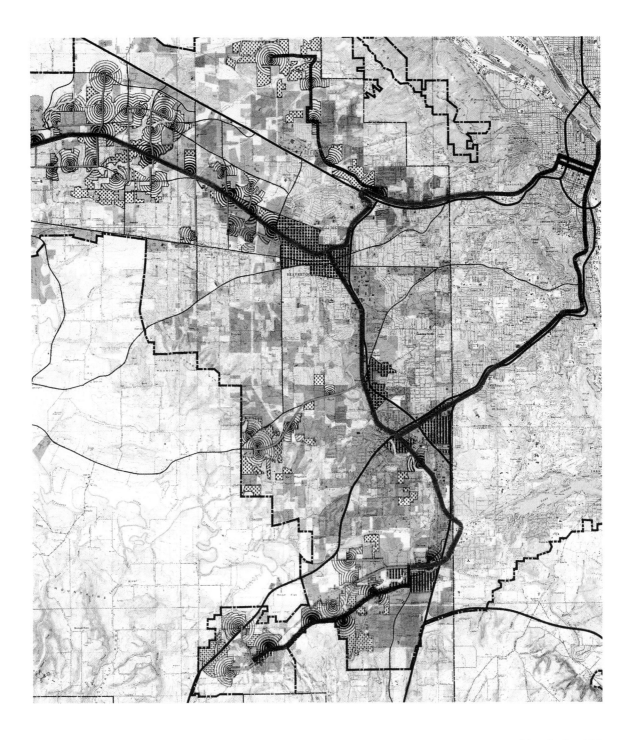

THE 1992 REGIONAL PLAN CALLED LUTRAQ—Making the Land Use, Transportation, Air Quality Connection—was sponsored by 1000 Friends of Oregon to pose alternatives to building a $200 million beltway around the west side of Portland, Oregon. LUTRAQ argued convincingly that expanding transit and planning for transit-oriented development (TOD) would create traffic solutions without building new highways.

1. THE REGIONAL LAND USE AND TRANSPORTATION CONNECTION

Highways make suburban sprawl possible and sprawl constantly requires more highways. The pattern feeds itself but never reaches resolution. To counter the negative spatial effects of sprawl, we must focus new development, redevelopment, and services within walkable, transit-served neighborhoods that are connected to larger concentrations of workplaces. Clustered services, adequate transit, walkable streets, and accessible local destinations serve not only youth, elderly, and low-income groups, but also working middle-class households in search of more convenient and affordable lifestyles. Metropolitan coordination and framework plans are necessary to integrate local land use with regional transportation investments.

2. FAIR HOUSING AND 'DECONCENTRATING' POVERTY

We won't solve the problems of the urban poor in the ghetto alone. For a region to function effectively, each jurisdiction within the metropolis must provide its fair share of affordable housing. This is true in terms of equity or plain economic efficiency. Policies supporting regional fair-housing distribution not only provide opportunities for the urban poor to move closer to the new job centers, but are also necessary to create the transportation efficiencies that result from the improved balance between jobs and housing. Certainly local strategies to improve inner-city neighborhoods are important, but they shouldn't displace regional strategies—the two

should reinforce each other. Deconcentrating dysfunctional pockets of poverty, providing access for the urban poor to suburban jobs, and beginning to mend the geographic isolation of economic classes in our society are essentially regional problems.

3. GREENLINES AND URBAN GROWTH BOUNDARIES

Environmental concerns for habitat, wetlands, open space, and farmlands, as well as the need for recreational open space, should be addressed in a regional framework rather than by piecemeal land acquisition and preservation. Preserving open space in a coherent manner can reinforce a development tendency toward more compact communities as well as the reuse and revitalization of many declining districts. Without clear, defensible limits to growth, investments in infrastructure and jobs will continue to sprawl. Environmental preservation and economic reinvestment can be wrapped in one regional policy.

4. REGIONAL TAX-BASE SHARING AND SOCIAL EQUITY

As long as basic local services are dependent on local property wealth, property tax-base sharing is a critical component of metropolitan stability. Property tax-base sharing creates equity in the provision of public services, breaks the intensifying sub-regional mismatch between social needs and tax resources, undermines the fiscal incentives that often drive sprawl, and ends intra-metropolitan

"[In Seattle], a new regional strategy resulted in the rejection of plans for a new 4,500-home suburb 20 miles from Seattle— exactly the kind of sprawl-and-flight phenomenon that national policies have so successfully encouraged. Seattle has begun to understand that its long-term viability can only be secured by acting like a city-region or a city-state, and therefore it has begun to knit together the destinies of city, suburbs, and the surrounding countryside."

DANIEL KEMMIS
The Good City and the Good Life

IN HAYWARD, CALIFORNIA (top), sprawling growth usurps hillsides and other natural lands. The traditional grid of Brigham City, Utah (bottom), contains growth while sparing the mountainsides and the fertile valley.

competition for tax base. Without regional tax-sharing provisions, inner-city economic decay will continue to spread. Local land-use decisions will continue to be balkanized and regionally dysfunctional.

5. URBAN SCHOOLS AND REGIONAL EDUCATION BALANCE

Viable urban schools are essential to healthy cities and balanced regional growth. Without them, only the rich, who can afford private schools, and the poor, who have no choice, will raise children in the city. The middle class continually abandons the city for better schools in the suburbs, shifting the region's economic and social balance. There are many ways to address this critical issue. For example, charter schools are not only a way of improving education standards for urban schools, but also can reinforce neighborhood participation and add to the human scale of a neighborhood. Another strategy is the urban school voucher. If school vouchers were regionally targeted toward inner-city and distressed districts, the poor would have more power over their school system, and the middle class would have an incentive to re-inhabit districts that need social and economic diversity. Physically zoned vouchers could help regain the balance between wealthy suburban school districts and poor city and inner-suburban districts.

Each of these regional strategies could stand alone. But the New Urbanism calls for a coordinated regional design that could synthesize these and other strategies and policies into a coherent regional form. Not doing so would be like designing your living room by leaving the furniture where the movers dropped it. The region, much like a neighborhood or street, can and should be "designed."

"The fractionalization of the city into separate political entities is one of the chief obstacles to urban design on the scale of the whole city."

PAUL SPREIREGEN
Urban Design:
The Architecture of
Towns and Cities

PETER CALTHORPE

Peter Calthorpe is a principal of Calthorpe Associates in Berkeley, California. He is a co-founder of CNU and a member of its Board of Directors, and the author of three books, including *The Next American Metropolis* (Princeton Architectural Press, 1993).

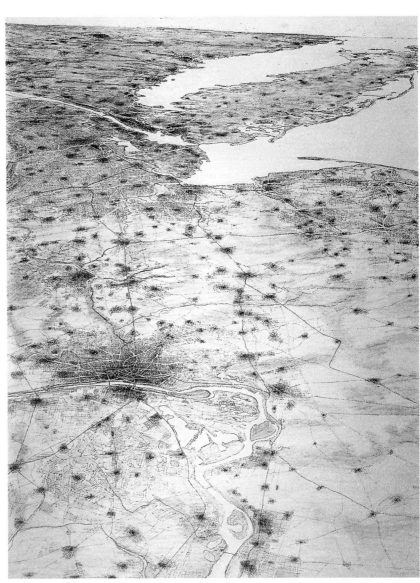

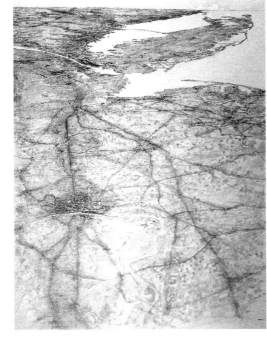

THREE VIEWS OF THE NORTHERN NEW JERSEY REGION: At present (top left); if built out under current development patterns (bottom left); and if built in compact patterns. The latter configuration preserves farmland by reinforcing cities, towns, and villages, each with their own center and edges.

Two

Metropolitan regions are finite places with geographic boundaries derived from topography, watersheds, coastlines, farmlands, regional parks, and river basins. The metropolis is made of multiple centers that are cities, towns, and villages, each with its own identifiable center and edges.

ROBERT D. YARO

Regionalism—the idea that metropolitan regions are stronger when they harmonize with their natural environments—is making more sense than ever. By preserving green space, protecting watersheds, investing in transit, and directing growth toward established areas, well-planned metropolitan regions are protecting their environmental health.

But they also are bolstering their economic health by providing amenities that attract entrepreneurial and creative people, particularly in technology and information-based industries. These people are increasingly "footloose" and will move their homes and businesses to regions that provide the best quality of life.

Most other U.S. metropolitan regions have rejected—or more correctly, neglected—the concept that regional attributes are critical to their well-being. But a growing number of places are rejecting sprawl and instead embracing this type of profitable regionalism.

One way regions can begin fostering this link between economic and ecological health is by marshaling a comprehensive plan; one that relates transit needs to vibrant downtowns, and that employs open space both as a recreational resource and a growth boundary. As Alexander Garvin observes in *The American City: What Works, What Doesn't*, the comprehensive regional plan "can be a powerful instrument for municipal improvement." In recent years, regional planning has become a higher priority still

"Whenever we make changes in our surroundings, we can all too easily shortchange ourselves. The way to avoid the danger is to start doing three things at once: Make sure that when we change a place, the change agreed upon nurtures our growth as capable and responsible people, while also protecting the natural environment, and developing jobs and homes enough for all."

TONY HISS
The Experience of Place

"To waste, to destroy, our natural resources, to skin and exhaust the land instead of using it so as to increase its usefulness, will result in undermining in the days of our children the very prosperity which we ought by right to hand down to them amplified and developed."

THEODORE ROOSEVELT
message to Congress, 1907

because regions need to meet federal standards for clean air and transportation. In the early 1990s, Sacramento, Seattle, and San Diego began preparing new metropolitan plans and organizing new growth in compact centers built around planned rail systems. These initiatives stem in part from the 1990 Clean Air Act Amendments and the 1991 Intermodal Surface Transportation Efficiency Act (ISTEA). Both pieces of legislation encourage land-use measures designed to attain clean-air standards.

To begin the pursuit of a regional plan, regions should first clearly define their own sense of identity. This is a process that begins as regions explore and celebrate their own natural, cultural, and architectural heritage.

We can see how this has evolved in Seattle. As the Seattle region has matured, it has identified styles for its architecture and public spaces that are specific to its setting. Many buildings combine locally harvested materials with Native American, maritime, industrial, and vernacular designs. The city has dedicated a major city park, Discovery Park, as a preserve of the native Puget Sound landscape. The proposed Mountains-to-Sound Greenway would connect the spine of the Cascade Mountains to the east with Puget Sound to the west, protecting historic and natural features along the route. The regional economy has become identified with exported products; not just timber, but airplanes, software, and a gourmet coffee company that has become ubiquitous. Despite the usual problems associated with sprawl, an increasing number of built places in this corner of the Northwest look as

though they belong. Now that the state has provided the framework of urban growth boundaries (UGBs), the region is proceeding to the next step. It is developing planning responses and funding transportation infrastructure that will ultimately preserve wetlands, prevent flooding, and spare distant forests and mountains the encroachment of urbanization.

HOW TO INITIATE AND PURSUE
A REGIONAL PLAN

To succeed in efforts to develop metropolitan plans, the citizens of a region must begin by registering broad public concern about threats to natural or cultural heritage, or to economic prospects. They must develop a consensus based upon a compelling and widely shared vision for a better future.

Regional governments are not essential to implement metropolitan strategies. Yet some form of regional governance is necessary. This can be provided by a civic group with powerful business or community leadership, such as New York's Regional Plan Association (RPA), Chicago's Metropolitan Planning Council, or Pittsburgh's Allegheny Conference. In San Diego, the San Diego County Association of Governments (SANDAG) has helped lead an effort to preserve 172,000 acres of critical wildlife habitat.

Regional service districts, such as New York's Palisades Interstate Park Commission, or Boston's Massachusetts Water Resources Authority, can promote sensible planning in the name of protecting a vital resource. In upstate New York, efforts to protect New York City's water supply have led to an agreement between the city and upstate communities to manage growth and protect land in the watershed. As a result of taking the initiative to safeguard its water quality, the city is saving $6 billion—the cost of a new filtration plant. In San Francisco, the Public Utilities Commission spent more than $2 million and five years on a plan to manage the 63,000-acre Peninsula and Alameda watersheds to preserve water quality, but also to conserve significant buffers to urbanization in the Bay Area.

Regional planning and governance can be provided by a regional council, such as the Minneapolis–St. Paul's Metropolitan Council, or by a regional government, such as Portland's Metro, created in 1979 as the nation's first elected metropolitan government. Regional planning authorities such as the Cape Cod Commission and the Tahoe Regional Planning Agency (whose authority straddles the California–Nevada border to include the entire Lake Tahoe basin) have also taken steps to integrate the design of urban areas with the preservation of open places.

Successful regions must direct most new employment and population to compact centers accessible to regional rail systems. This requires improving transit networks while proposals for new or expanded highways are put on hold. Rail systems should focus on a vibrant 24-hour regional central business district (CBD), which must also contain major cultural, educational, governmental, retail, entertainment, and employment activities; have lively residential neighborhoods representing all income levels within or near the CBD; preserve the historic fabric of these neighborhoods and the CBD; and provide high-quality public spaces and street life.

Since 1980, cities such as Baltimore, Cleveland, Denver, Milwaukee, Portland, Seattle, and Sacramento have formed a nucleus of successful regions featuring these attributes. That is half the equation. The other half, only now beginning in cities like Philadelphia and San Diego, is to define and protect the open-space systems needed to create green limits to growth.

"It is thrifty to prepare today for the wants of tomorrow."
AESOP
The Ant and the Grasshopper

A REGION AT RISK

Equity   Environment

Increasing gap between rich and poor

Quality of life

Wasteful consumption of resources

Sluggish "boom & bust" growth

Economy

Greensward →
Mobility →
Centers →
Workforce →
Governance →

A COMPETITIVE REGION

Equity   Environment

Improving prosperity for all

Increased quality of life

A healthy regional ecosystem

Vibrant sustainable growth

Economy

ROBERT D. YARO

Robert D. Yaro is executive director of the Regional Plan Association in New York City and a co-author of *Rural By Design: Maintaining Small Town Character* (APA Planners Press, 1994) and *A Region at Risk* (Island Press, 1996).

IN THE NEW YORK CITY METROPOLITAN REGION, the Regional Plan
Association employs images like these to show citizens the results of alternative growth
scenarios. Here a typical suburban commercial strip is contrasted with more compact
and aesthetically pleasing development.

Regional Planning: The New York Experience

For more than 75 years, the nonprofit Regional Plan Association (RPA) has worked effectively in the New York–New Jersey–Connecticut metropolitan region, the nation's largest. In 1929, RPA's landmark *Plan for New York* (the world's first comprehensive metropolitan plan) proposed the creation of a vast regional park and parkway system. By 1950 this was largely in place, but postwar sprawl soon outpaced many of its measures and benefits.

To keep up with the demands posed by Baby Boom–fueled growth, RPA's second regional plan of 1968 proposed major expansion of the region's open-space system. It also suggested creating a network of satellite centers, linked by a revitalized regional rail system, to accommodate the region's rapidly decentralizing population and economy.

As a result of these strategies, paired with $25 billion to rebuild the rail system, New York City and the region's 12 "regional downtowns" are linked today by modernized transit that carries more than five million passengers daily, nearly one-half of total U.S. ridership. These "re-magnetized" urban centers contain more than half the region's jobs, a far higher share than in any other large U.S. metropolitan area.

Despite these considerable efforts, the rate of New York–area sprawl is still rising. Since 1965, the population of metropolitan New York has increased only 13 percent, but urbanized land swelled by 61 percent. For this reason, *A Region at Risk*, RPA's Third Regional Plan of 1996, aims to regain a grip on this region, which comprises three states, 31 counties, and about 2,000 different governments. The plan calls for a 4-million-acre Metropolitan Greensward. A network of 11 protected "regional reserves" would encompass mountains, estuaries, farms, and forests, as well as hundreds of rural villages. A regional greenway system could link these to "re-greened" urban centers. When completed, this preserved network of public and private lands will provide a permanent "green edge" to growth—a *de facto* urban growth boundary—ranging from New York Harbor to the Appalachian Highlands.

—ROBERT YARO

Three

The metropolis has a necessary and fragile relationship to its agrarian hinterland and natural landscapes. The relationship is environmental, economic, and cultural. Farmland and nature are as important to the metropolis as the garden is to the house.

RANDALL ARENDT

In this era of modern agriculture, do efforts to save farmland amount to little more than a sentimental gesture? The answer is that saving farmland and other agricultural land remains crucial to the health of metropolitan communities. Despite the onslaught of sprawl, farms remain a major economic, natural, and social factor near and even within urban America. Efforts to preserve such agricultural lands are vital to both the economic and natural balance within many metropolitan regions. Many acres of productive land can still be saved in a way that has a positive effect on the shape of development.

One third of all American farms—that's 640,000 farms—are located in the nation's 320 Metropolitan Statistical Areas (MSAs), or areas with at least 50,000 residents. Covering 159 million acres, these farms account for 20 percent of the country's harvested cropland. In the Northeast, half the farms are in MSAs. In the Pacific region, the proportion is two-thirds. According to *American Farmland* magazine, farms in metro areas produce 79 percent of our fruits, 69 percent of our vegetables, and 52 percent of our milk.

In addition to safeguarding the productivity of these farms, we must conserve the special relationship between urban areas and their hinterlands. The rural hinterlands are loosely defined as those areas where less than 15 percent of the land has been developed for "non-resource" purposes, such as suburban development. The hinterlands provide much more than breathing room for metropolitan areas. More basically, they

"Our farms are in danger of becoming subdivisions or shopping malls. We can't sit back and take our farms, and the food they supply, for granted."
DAN GLICKMAN
U.S. Secretary of Agriculture

 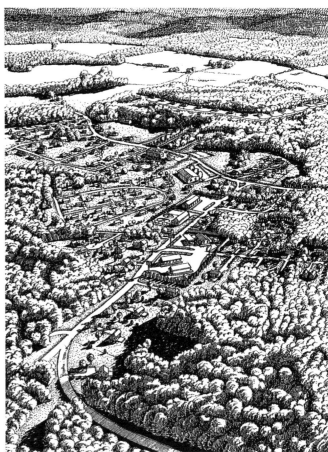

THREE AERIAL VIEWS
of the same landscape.
Today's view (above left).
After conventional development (above right). After
cluster development
(facing page).

supply and protect high-quality drinking water. Cities such as Boston, New York, and San Francisco realized this early and purchased or set aside vast acreage of land in their hinterlands for reservoirs and associated watersheds. The hinterlands also improve the region's quality of life and its economic base by providing opportunities for outdoor recreation and tourism.

Finally, the hinterlands can be the home of small-scale organic farms, which are compatible with residential living. These supply flowers, meat, and produce to corner groceries, farmers' markets, and area restaurants, enlivening these public spaces with a sense of regional identity and pride.

Between the metropolitan center and the hinterlands, there exists an intermediate suburban zone where 15 to 85 percent of the land has been developed. The band occupied by this intermediate zone often extends 20 to 40 miles from the outer edge of the older suburbs to the inner edge of the rural hinterlands. Even these suburban areas are sometimes highly productive and should be protected against sprawling development. They typically contain a significant acreage of farmland and woodlands, as well as miles of riparian habitat.

Without effective regional growth-management strategies, both the hinterlands and the intermediate zone remain vulnerable to future waves of sprawl.

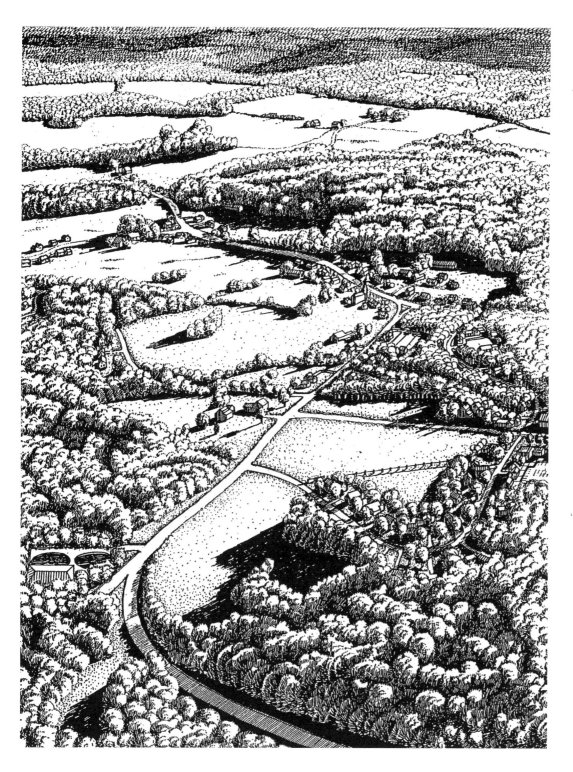

"Big cities and countrysides can get along well together. Big cities need real countryside close by. And countryside—from man's point of view—needs big cities, with all their diverse opportunities and productivity, so human beings can be in a position to appreciate the rest of the natural world instead of to curse it."

JANE JACOBS
The Death and Life of American Cities

"Asphalt is the last crop you'll grow on the land."
BILL GAY
Colorado rancher

"Town and country must
be married, and out of
this joyous union will
spring a new hope, a new
life, a new civilization."
EBENEZER HOWARD

In recent years, many techniques have been developed to preserve open lands. Most are designed to compensate landowners who might otherwise sell their land for development. These techniques include urban growth boundaries (UGBs), transfer of development rights (TDRs), purchase of development rights (PDRs), right-to-farm laws, and the establishment of land trusts or of organizations that accept donations of conservation easements.

In any given community, these special compensatory mechanisms might protect a few parcels of open space. Yet society's ability to conserve more land is crippled by existing suburban zoning densities. These typically range from one-half acre to five acres per dwelling. No land-conservation efforts will be effective unless the basic groundwork—the zoning regulations—are changed.

Rezoning to preserve rural resources and uses involves two strategies. They work best when paired. The first strategy is to adjust zoning to create minimum tract sizes large enough to support farming and ranching. The minimum amount of land needed to farm or ranch varies dramatically. In the Pacific Northwest, with wet climate and rich soils, five acres can support a farm. In the temperate Northeast, one can profit from a celery farm of about 20 acres. The ranches of the arid West require much larger parcels running into thousands of acres.

The other strategy involves creating urban-design regulations and incentives that cluster development onto a much smaller portion of a parcel than would otherwise be occupied. This technique is sometimes called *conservation subdivision design*. Such clustering will not prevent development from becoming dispersed. However, in concert with planning to identify important lands to conserve, this strategy can reserve as much as 70 percent of developable land as open space. With advanced planning, these pieces of land can be knit together into a greenbelt or open-space network.

Under conventional development scenarios, the first 5 percent of development often ruins 50 percent of the countryside. If you take a small amount of development, even just three buildings, and put them in the middle of a farm field, you effectively destroy the field. If you put these buildings at the edge of the field, or behind some trees, you can preserve the character and the function of that landscape.

We should embrace these imaginative ways to accommodate inevitable growth. The alternative is too dismal to contemplate: letting development take the course of least resistance, through a framework of conventional codes that will produce endless acres of low-density sprawl, each proposed and approved independently, and eventually spreading over mile after square mile of countryside.

RANDALL ARENDT

Randall Arendt is the vice president for conservation planning at the Natural Lands Trust in Media, Pennsylvania, and the author of *Rural By Design* (APA Planners Press, 1994), *Growing Greener: Putting Conservation into Local Codes* (Island Press, 1999), and *The Design Characteristics of Hamlets, Villages and Traditional Small Town Neighborhoods* (APA Planning Advisory Service, 1999).

AN AGRICULTURAL COMMUNITY IN NEWTON, UTAH (top), built on a tight grid, preserves farmland. Under conventional development scenarios (bottom), the first 5 percent of development can ruin 50 percent of the landscape. Even just three buildings placed in the middle of a farm field effectively destroys the field.

Saving Agricultural Lands Through Cluster Development

Local officials in Pennsylvania have discovered that clustered development can work to conserve agricultural lands and important woodland habitat. Developed by the Natural Lands Trust for the state's Department of Conservation and Natural Resources, a planning education program called "Growing Greener" involves making small but significant changes to local comprehensive plans, subdivision ordinances, and zoning ordinances. Under Growing Greener, these three layers of planning and zoning are harnessed into a single force that allows development to be clustered on part of a piece of land.

When coordinated over a period of years, this approach, also known as conservation subdivision design, identifies the land most important to conserve throughout a municipality. By following the principles of Growing Greener, developers can quickly become leading conservationists, as each new subdivision adds another link to the community's open-space system. Best of all, this can be achieved without controversial downzoning, costly subsidies, or complicated density transfers.

By applying the Growing Greener principles, Lower Makefield Township in Bucks County, Pennsylvania, has saved 500 acres of prime farmland in the last five years. Moreover, the township has avoided costly "takings" claims because conservation subdivision design allows full-density development in every subdivision.

Growing Greener also means growing denser. Our biggest challenge may be to convince Americans to accept the compact, "centered" growth that is necessary to preserve open lands. We must broadcast the facts concerning the huge costs of financing low-density sprawl, as well as the benefits of attractive, livable, and accessible urban centers.

—RANDALL ARENDT

Four

Development patterns should not blur or eradicate the edges of the metropolis. Infill development within existing areas conserves environmental resources, economic investment, and social fabric, while reclaiming marginal and abandoned areas. Metropolitan regions should develop strategies to encourage such infill development over peripheral expansion.

JACKY GRIMSHAW

Only a few metropolitan regions have been able to grapple with growth and suburban sprawl by forming effective regional governments. But numerous other regions are finding that grass-roots efforts—led by citizens, civic organizations, environmental groups, and churches, frequently in coalitions—can work toward regional planning goals that focus on reviving city centers as a strategy to curtail sprawl.

The New Urbanism is a key element of this approach. I learned of the New Urbanism in 1992 when my organization, the Chicago-based Center for Neighborhood Technology (CNT), was assisting residents of the West Garfield Park community along the city's Lake Street elevated train. Our goal was to convince the Chicago Transit Authority to rehab rather than demolish the deteriorating line. Running from Oak Park in the western suburbs, through the Loop, the Lake Street "El" was privately built in 1890. Publicly owned since 1947, it had faced declining ridership and station closings since then. It appeared to be redundant because another line ran parallel a few miles away. Sometimes you could walk downtown faster because its track was plagued by "slow zones" that also posed safety problems. Although fewer than half of the households in West Garfield had access to a car, only 6 percent of residents commuted to work on the Lake Street El. The Transit Authority was naturally reluctant to spend the $400 million required for repairs. At the same time, the West Garfield Park community was up in arms about the prospect of losing the line and its

NEW DEVELOPMENT
PROPOSED AROUND
CHICAGO'S "GREEN
LINE" (below) will bring
services into a decaying
neighborhood while revitalizing transit. The transit
connection helps people
decrease their spending on
cars and thus frees income
for housing. Special mortgage packages are helping
homebuyers who have
access to transit qualify
for larger loans.

Pulaski station, but realized that some brilliant solution was needed to save it.

Then we discovered the New Urbanist concept of transit-oriented development (TOD). This involves zoning the areas around transit stations—too often wasted on surface parking lots—for compact development that provides services for the neighborhood and for commuters. This was a new idea at the time. The only other central-city application of these transit-oriented design principles was at the Fruitvale station of Bay Area Rapid Transit (BART) in Oakland, California. In Chicago, we quickly recognized the opportunity to revitalize transit and a neighborhood simultaneously.

The challenge was to make this sort of public and private investment appealing within a low-income neighborhood. Between 1950 and 1990, the population of West Garfield Park dropped from 60,000 to 24,000. This was once a thriving industrial area. But many of the industries, including Schwinn Bicycle, had moved away. The residential blocks on side streets were pocked with vacant lots. Forty percent of the land around the Pulaski station was vacant. The neighborhood did host

a regional shopping area, but it lacked such basic services as a grocery store and a family restaurant. Nevertheless, 118,000 people—the population of a small city—still lived within a half-mile of the Pulaski station.

To address these issues, CNT and Douglas Farr, a CNU-member architect, led a community planning charrette. Through a partnership among the city, the Transit Authority, and a coalition of community activists, funds became available through the federal Intermodal Surface Transportation Efficiency Act (ISTEA) for other planning. Under what came to be called the Community Green Line Initiative, the Transit Authority agreed not only to rebuild the line, but to build a new station with room for a day-care center and other privately run neighborhood services. The City declared a redevelopment area aimed to attract neighborhood services within a quarter-mile around the Pulaski transit stop.

In 1994, the line was closed for reconstruction. Consolidated with another line and renamed the Green Line, it reopened in 1996 and is just beginning to surpass its former level of ridership. The

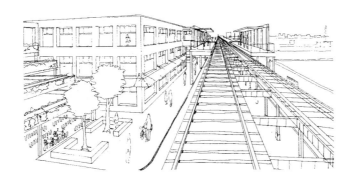

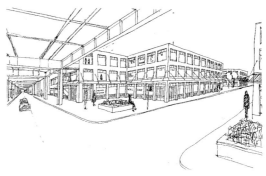

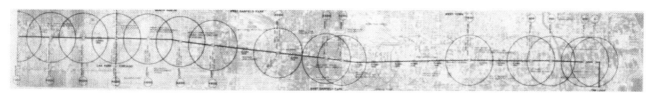

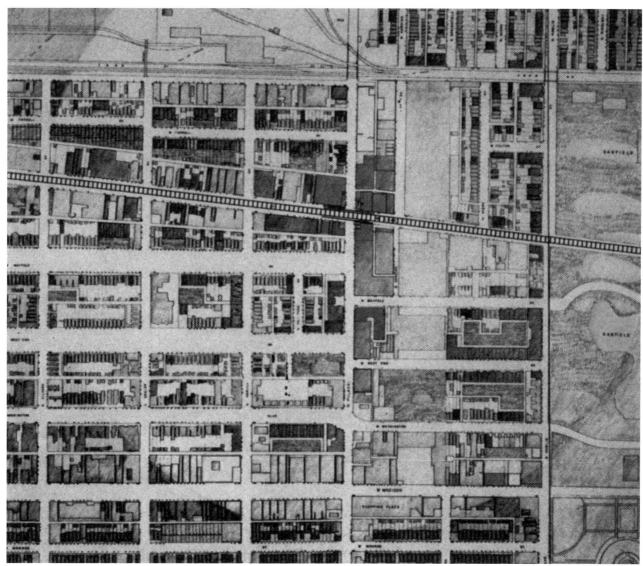

THE COMMUNITY GREEN LINE INITIATIVE PLAN for a typical station, West Garfield Park, an area where the population dropped from 60,000 to 24,000 in a generation (bottom). Circles in the top drawing represent a five-minute/quarter-mile walk to the station and the areas with highest potential for transit-oriented development (TOD).

VIEW OF WEST
GARFIELD PARK with
new Pulaski station to the
left. Lenders have established
preferential programs for
homebuyers in neighbor-
hoods with transit-oriented
development plans. Such
programs help level the field
between city and suburb.

JACKY GRIMSHAW
CNU board member Jacky Grimshaw is coordinator of transportation and air quality
programs for the Chicago-based Center for Neighborhood Technology.

new Pulaski station has become the model for rebuilding other stations along the Green Line. In addition, the Transit Authority has agreed to land swaps to make properties available immediately around the station. These are now slated to be redeveloped to create a good-sized grocery store, pharmacy, and other services. There is talk of adding movie theaters, which have long been missing from the area.

Another goal is to create opportunities for people who live in the neighborhood to start their own businesses or to acquire franchises. Local lending institutions and foundations have agreed to establish a special loan program for entrepreneurs in neighborhoods that have TOD plans in place. A nonprofit community development corporation is building new homes on West Garfield's vacant lots. Developed in cooperation with the Federal National Mortgage Association (Fannie Mae), a pioneering concept called a location-efficient mortgage (LEM) may make these houses more affordable. The idea is simple: If you live within a transit-oriented neighborhood, you spend less money on cars. Recognizing the difference this makes to your household income, the lending institution may

give you a bigger loan. One estimate is that this can leverage an additional $54,000 for a borrower to purchase a home. Fannie Mae has approved our regional experiment for the LEM. If the concept goes national—and it has strong support from the White House—it will benefit low-to-middle-income homebuyers who seek to live in denser neighborhoods served by transit and walkable retail. The West Garfield LEM will also include a deeply discounted transit pass for homebuyers.

Taken as a whole, this program addresses what some view as a major cause of sprawl: the competitive edge of the suburbs. If you're shopping for a home, you will often find it easier to procure a mortgage in the suburbs. You may have the prospect of convenient services and transportation, or you may even live closer to your job or to business opportunities in the suburbs. But your transportation choice may be limited to driving your car alone down the freeway. This adds high transportation costs to that "affordable" house, making it potentially more expensive than one in a location-efficient neighborhood.

The Green Line project seeks to level the playing field between city and suburban housing choices. It does so by improving housing, providing an advantage through lending institutions, including top-notch mass transit, and both protecting and creating jobs. When walkable, working-class city neighborhoods are revitalized, all residents of a region can benefit because the entire region will offer more housing and transit choices as well as improved livability.

Odd Bedfellows Make Strong Coalitions in Chicago

In the Chicago region, citizen groups are transcending municipal lines to develop the type of regional strategies that fractured governments can't achieve. Among them:

One coalition seeks to stop major toll-road expansions because these new roads are catalysts for urban disinvestment and sprawl. This group is composed of the Environmental Law and Policy Center of the Midwest, Business and Professional People for the Public Interest, the American Lung Association, the Chicagoland Bicycle Federation, the Illinois Chapter of the Sierra Club, and the Center for Neighborhood Technology.

The disparities caused by sprawl are not only being challenged by nonprofits and citizen groups. The Commercial Club of Chicago is sponsoring the Metropolis Project—a new Burnham plan for the 21st century. This plan, *Preparing Metropolitan Chicago for the 21st Century*, embodies New Urbanist principles as it seeks to address issues of poverty, housing, transportation, pollution, race, and jobs.

In addition, the faith-based Metropolitan Alliance of Congregations is educating citizen leaders and congregations in Cook and Will counties about the social, economic, and environmental conditions in the region, and telling them how to influence decision makers regarding land use and transportation planning.

In the area of housing development and policies, groups as diverse as the Metropolitan Planning Council, the Commercial Club, the Leadership Council for Metropolitan Open Communities, Regional Action Project 2000+, the Chicago Rehab Network, and dozens of community development corporations understand the problems caused by the mismatch between housing and jobs. They are doing everything from promoting federal public-housing reform to focusing on dispersing the isolated, high-density pockets of poverty by creating mixed-income communities.

A citizen group called the Chicagoland Transportation and Air Quality Commission created the *Citizen Transportation Plan for Northeastern Illinois —The $650 Billion Decision*. This long-range transportation plan lays out a policy and planning framework for transportation decisions for the next 25 years. The plan also advocates infill projects and redevelopment in existing communities, strong farmland protection policies, transit-oriented development, and the redevelopment of industrial brownfields.

The group of citizens who helped craft the transportation vision understood that the continued disinvestment in the city and inner suburbs creates pressures to develop farmland in other parts of the region. The Citizen Plan has now been endorsed by 139 organizations and municipalities. If implemented, it would begin to moderate sprawl.

—JACKY GRIMSHAW

Why Cities Matter to New Urbanism

I was drawn to the principles of New Urbanism upon hearing about them in 1993. The use of the word "new" affixed to "urbanism" suggested freshness, vitality, and energy. The concepts of livability, sustainability, small-scale neighborhood development, walkability, and more intense utilization of public transportation were appealing to someone like me, who had spent decades fighting sprawl.

But I am also a lover of "old urbanism," a child of the city. I have spent my entire adult life working in the core city, where development patterns already exist. I grew up in a working-class neighborhood with sidewalks, front porches, and stickball in the street. Today I live within two blocks of my office, and walk to restaurants and go to pop concerts a few blocks away.

My fascination with New Urbanism has as much to do with my reaction to the so-called decline of cities, which has been reinforced in the media's negative perceptions of the urban core in the last 30 to 40 years. To many people, urban means poor folk, too many minorities, crime, drugs, and unstable families. It means overcrowding, traffic jams, limited open space, and substandard schools and facilities. It means political confusion, abandoned shopping centers, and even abandoned neighborhoods.

Yet cities have tremendous assets that are often overlooked. They are the home of great medical centers, colleges and universities, cultural facilities, government buildings, employment centers, and the basic infrastructure of streets, utilities, and public transportation—not to mention the wonderful diversity of people that reflects what America is all about.

These resources are struggling against the forces that draw people and investment away from the core. The result has been a tremendous flight of middle Americans chasing the "American Dream," coupled with meaningless municipal boundaries that have not only accelerated physical abandonment, but also isolated core cities, socially and politically. There are some notable successes, such as Portland, Seattle, Denver, Milwaukee, Charlotte, and Charleston. Even in these cities there are still at-risk neighborhoods with complex social and physical conditions.

CAN PHYSICAL DESIGN OVERCOME PROBLEMS OF THE CITY? Computer-generated photomontage shows proposed streetscape improvements around the historic Fox movie palace in downtown Oakland, California. Cyber-improvements include new street trees, lighting, bus lanes, and infill buildings.

There is a real challenge here for New Urbanism. If the goal of the New Urbanism is to rekindle the American Dream (admittedly an ephemeral and spiritual goal) by building settlements that encourage community, livability, convenience, decent housing, and preservation of the environment, then a significant thrust of this movement must focus on the existing core city. This especially means infill development of at-risk neighborhoods, whether in urban or first-ring suburban areas.

The Congress for the New Urbanism has the brainpower, resources, values, and design principles necessary to meet the challenge of infill, core city development. But there are challenges we need to address first:

The initial problems are not always a matter of physical design. They involve investment patterns, job security, school quality, racial discrimination, and the political complexities that produce tangled bureaucracies and ineffective zoning. We must recognize that working in the inner city does not lend itself to quick-fix solutions. It may require years of work to change something like bad zoning laws. I have seen at-risk neighborhoods in Charlotte begin to turn around with nothing more than better police patrol, better newspaper coverage, a neighborhood watch program, or a new elementary school principal.

We must think incrementally—street by street, block by block, neighborhood by neighborhood. Sometimes it may be a simple improvement like a mini-park, a reformed slum landlord making improvements to his property, or an adaptive reuse of an abandoned shopping center. We must have the patience to see these incremental actions as a positive catalyst. The question is whether we commit to the long-term involvement required.

We should not assume we will be trusted in the inner city. We must ask whether we are prepared as architects, urban designers, and planners to work at gaining credibility with neighborhood activists, politicians, and the community. Often, we are seen as the enemy—we helped build the freeways that facilitated the exodus, we built the regional malls, we built suburbia.

Are we prepared to measure success in a different way? As important as physical renewal and revitalization is, the real success of revitalizing the old involves human dynamics. Do people feel like they are part of a place or a community? Has crime decreased measurably? Are children becoming better educated? Does the promise of the American Dream seem real to more people?

The New Urbanism has already made a substantial contribution to the movement to control urban sprawl. But if we take on the challenges of infill development and help to make revitalized cities commonplace, we will move this Congress to a new level.

—HARVEY GANTT

HARVEY GANTT

A former mayor of Charlotte, North Carolina, Harvey Gantt is a board member of the Congress for the New Urbanism. He is an architect and partner in the firm of Gantt Huberman in Charlotte.

IN THE NORTHWEST CORRIDOR BEYOND PERTH, AUSTRALIA,
the proposed Jindalee Town would structure new growth into neighborhoods and towns around a rail line.

Five

Where appropriate, new development contiguous to urban boundaries should be organized as neighborhoods and districts, and be integrated with the existing urban pattern. Noncontiguous development should be organized as towns and villages with their own urban edges, and planned for a jobs/housing balance, not as bedroom suburbs.

WENDY MORRIS

As a basis for managing growth within a region, the New Urbanism provides an excellent framework for weaving new neighborhoods into the urban pattern and for creating self-contained, mixed-use towns and villages outside the city. In both cases, it's critical that we view and plan for the region as a whole.

DIRECTING GROWTH INTO CLUSTERING NEIGHBORHOODS

Planning new, urban extensions, known in Australia as regional or urban structuring, involves analyzing the existing urban structure around a site and highlighting town and neighborhood centers, key regional attractions and destinations, and school and community facilities. This analysis, combined with an analysis of the proposed growth area and beyond, allows us to identify existing points of connection, existing and planned infrastructure, site features, barriers, and long-term urban edges. It addresses how people go about their daily activities. Where are the neighborhood and town centers? Where is the public transit system, and how well is it accessed? Are the towns and neighborhoods well-connected, or are they separated? How does the project site connect to adjacent and nearby neighborhoods? Are neighborhood centers appropriately distributed, or are they limiting each other's potential? What factors about local economies, histories, politics, and jurisdictions could impede a project's success?

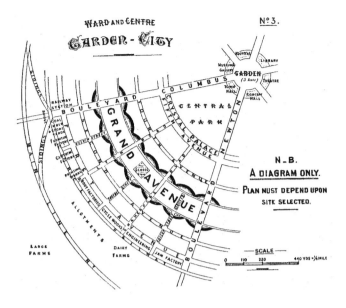

"A lack of boundary simply creates a kind of chaotic environment which none of us feel very proprietary towards—neither the residents nor the rest of the community nor certainly outsiders.... Making boundaries is akin to stabilizing the city so that its virtues remain across generations rather than seeming to be temporary, not like those houses that gather feet and go away. So create edges and boundaries. Make them very strong. They are akin to making a defined understanding of the particular place, activities, techniques of building and systems of service. We must not start with the geometry but with the user."

DONLYN LYNDON

Places

From this analysis, we can design a regional structure, showing the site and its role in the context of existing and future development. We can also identify the strengths and weaknesses of the existing urban structure with the aim of using new development to help solve problems such as inefficient transit connections.

REGIONAL STRUCTURING

The key planning goal is to concentrate compatible residential and work populations within clusters of walkable neighborhoods to form towns, while locating less compatible activities, such as heavy industry or extensive open spaces, in between or beyond these clusters. The relatively dense and commercial town centers should be located around a major public transit interchange or at intersections of major traffic routes.

Neighborhood edges should meld seamlessly, except where natural barriers, large green spaces, freeways, or other boundaries provide a prominent edge. It's important to design with the features of the land to define urban boundaries and establish a sense of identity. A ring of green around every neighborhood isn't necessary.

If we design beyond the site to an urban edge —at least to the edge of the outer neighborhoods of a town cluster—we begin to see the benefit of regional planning for infrastructure, especially for roads and public transit. A similar approach to regional, town, and neighborhood structuring can be used for proposed urban areas that have no connection to existing urban areas.

EMPLOYMENT TRENDS AND JOBS/HOUSING BALANCE

New Urbanist communities work well in generating employment opportunities in our post-industrial economy of small businesses, home-based businesses, digitally connected branches of large businesses, and part-time and multiple employment. To provide adequate opportunities for business and employment growth, I believe that as much as 30 percent of a mixed-use town or neighborhood core should accommodate different kinds of workplaces. The core also needs cafes and other services that support workers, as well as diverse building types with room for expansion and evolution.

DESIGNING URBAN EXPANSIONS

Many New Urbanist projects must be grafted onto fringes of conventional suburban development, in areas that have little in the way of services, retail shops, integrated workplaces, or sense of place. The new neighborhood creates a center for the existing residential community, and that community in turn provides critical early support for the center's businesses and services.

WHEN IS A NEW TOWN NECESSARY?
From my experience, three factors determine the need for new towns. The first is population size. For a mixed-use community to be self-sufficient, it needs a population and physical size that can support all the facets of urban life, such as homes, schools, shopping, jobs, and recreational opportunities, as well as community, medical, and government services.

The extent of self-sufficiency also depends on other factors, such as the degree of isolation; the attractiveness of neighboring urban areas for shopping, work, education, and culture; the extent of social diversity; and the sense of identity with and commitment to the local community. On the metropolitan fringe, between four and eight neighborhoods clustered around a town center can operate as a relatively self-contained community.

The size of a new, noncontiguous settlement depends on the region. In very remote rural areas, towns of a few thousand people have evolved to become relatively self-sufficient. By contrast, a relatively self-sufficient town within 60 miles of an existing metropolis may require from 30,000 to 100,000 or more people to overcome the strong commuting pull of the bigger city and the related resistance to commercial investment.

The question of size, structure, and sustainability is a critical area of investigation and debate for New Urbanists. Unrealistic claims have been made that small New Urbanist settlements surrounded by countryside are self-sufficient communities. While such towns and neighborhoods of a few hundred to a few thousand people may be very attractive and pleasant to live in, and may support some shops and workplaces, they also can generate much more auto travel than a well-planned neighborhood added to the edge of an existing urban area.

WENDY MORRIS

Wendy Morris is a principal of Ecologically Sustainable Design, an urban design firm in Victoria, Australia, that specializes in New Urbanism, mixed-use development, and the link between urban form and the post-industrial economy.

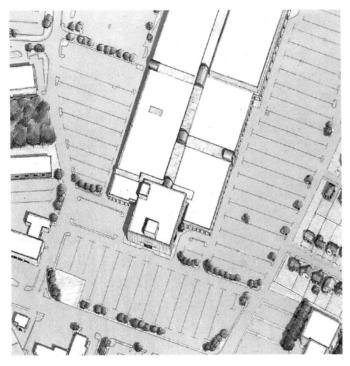

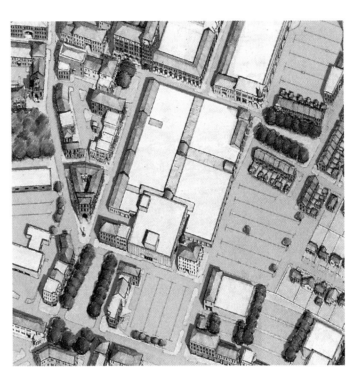

CURRENT

5 YEARS

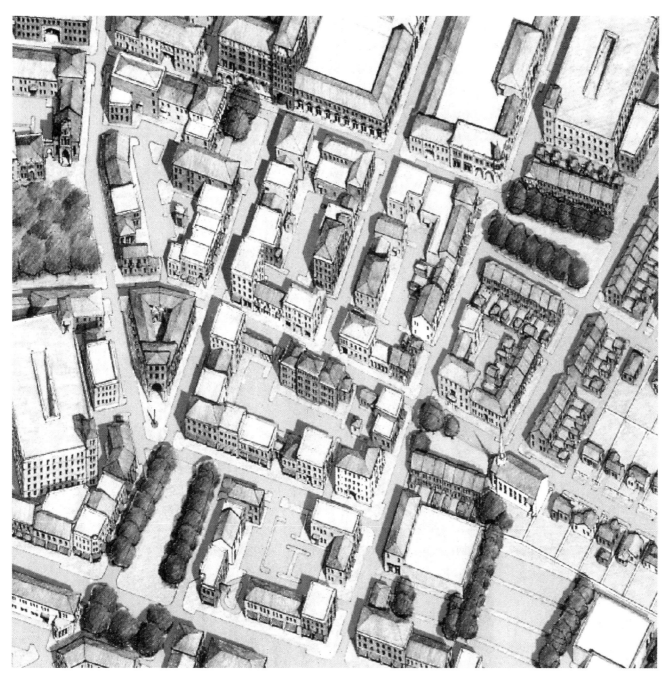

FUTURE

DESIGN FOR GRADUAL CHANGE: Redevelopment of Eastgate Mall in Chattanooga, Tennessee. In 1997 (far left), the mall was nearly empty. Within nine months, a town square replaced the parking lot and the mall was "turned inside-out" toward the street (middle). The mall is now 90 percent leased. Plan (above) shows sweeping changes proposed over a generation to reclaim empty spaces with buildings and public places.

Six

The development and redevelopment of towns and cities
should respect historical patterns, precedents, and boundaries.

STEPHANIE BOTHWELL

In Colonial New England, towns were laid out collectively by the community, and the
boundaries extended only as far as the town meeting bell could be heard. The building
of homes and businesses once was focused around the "heart" of the community—
the town green was its cultural, economic, and spiritual center. From the local hilltop,
people could see their community laid out and could understand it.

Viewed from above, America's landscape now shows the enormous changes that
human habitation has wrought over hundreds of years. In some places, we can still
recognize the piece that each town and surrounding farmsteads played in shaping the
pattern of that region's landscape. We can see the natural and manmade boundaries
that meet at the bases of mountains and edges of rivers, and the precedents that give
us bearings within patterns such as street grids and downtown cores.

What is overwhelmingly apparent from this perspective are the breaks with the
traditional historic patterns and precedents of development. They include tears in
the urban fabric—abandoned lots, public housing projects, and "megadevelopments"
created by urban renewal and highways. They also include rends in the wilderness,
where nature has been torn at the edges and patched with development. The suburban
patterns of alternating strip malls and circuitous street systems may be visually seductive,
but they suggest an underlying lack of order, an endlessly repetitive, piecemeal
approach to development.

"Where you find a people who believe that man and nature are indivisible, and that survival and health are contingent upon an understanding of nature and her processes, these societies will be very different from ours, as will their towns, cities, and landscapes.

The hydraulic civilizations, the good farmer through time, the vernacular city builders, have all displayed this acuity."

IAN MCHARG
Design with Nature

Towns and cities built before World War II followed traditional city and town planning principles. Historic towns and cities, such as Annapolis, Boston, Charleston, and San Francisco, as well as the planned communities of the first third of this century, such as Coral Gables, Shaker Heights, and Forest Hills, all demonstrated how traditional principles and their elements of pattern, precedent, and boundary could be used to create highly successful and enduring public and private realms.

After World War II, these principles were all but abandoned. Traditional neighborhood building, which had been characterized by moderately high densities and diversity of land use, was replaced by radically transformed patterns that had more to do with promoting individuality through separation and commercial interests and less to do with building community. Responsibility for the creation of

WHEN FREEWAYS and overscaled development rip apart the traditional scale of city streets, the damage is much more difficult to repair than simply filling in vacant lots with new houses and businesses. Fortunately, some communities wisely chose to keep their fabric intact, and this has spurred new investment.

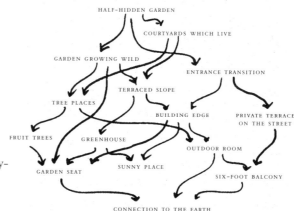

"I am the Lorax. I speak
for the trees. I speak for
the trees, because the
trees have no tongues."
DR. SEUSS
The Lorax

places shifted from an individual and community-based process to our present model shaped predominantly by specialists: architects, developers, engineers, landscape architects, and planners.

Among the notable responses to this pattern of development was Jane Jacobs's *Death and Life of Great American Cities*, published in 1961, which signaled a renewed interest in urban neighborhoods. From then on, the preservation movement, which opposed new development that threatened to tear down historic neighborhoods, forced designers, planners, and politicians to revisit traditional neighborhood design principles.

Throughout time, people have developed vernacular design and building practices in response to their needs, desires, and environments. Each community shared a local vision and language of how to build their world, as well as more universal principles about patterns, precedents, and boundaries. They shared common customs and culture that led them to create places that were part of a larger, coherent, ordered, and intrinsically beautiful whole. Christopher Alexander calls this intuitive knowledge "the timeless way of building" in his 1979 book of the same title.

In another of Alexander's books, *A Pattern Language*, he concludes that "no pattern is an isolated entity. Each pattern can exist in a work only to the extent that it is supported by other patterns: the larger patterns in which it is embedded, the patterns of the same size that surround it, and the

smaller patterns which are embedded in it. This is a fundamental view of the world. It says that when you build a thing you are not merely building the thing in isolation but must also repair the world around it, and within it, so that the larger world at that one place becomes more coherent, and more whole; and the thing which you make takes its place in the web of nature, as you make it."

In a sense, we have come full circle. Viewing our landscape from above, we can see that historic development patterns produced orderly, coherent, livable communities. In building and rebuilding towns and cities, we should respect the historical patterns, precedents, and boundaries that made earlier settlements flourish.

"There is one timeless way
of building. It is thousands
of years old, and the same
today as it has always been.
The great traditional buildings of the past, the villages
and tents and temples in
which man feels at home,
have always been made
by people who were very
close to the center of this
way. And as you see, this
way will lead anyone who
looks for it to buildings
which are themselves as
ancient in their form
as the trees and hills, and
as our faces are."
CHRISTOPHER
ALEXANDER
The Timeless Way of Building

STEPHANIE BOTHWELL

Stephanie Bothwell is director of the American Institute of Architects' Center for Livable Communities. She has taught at the Rhode Island School of Design and the Auburn University College of Architecture. She formerly was senior landscape architect for the City of Boston's Neighborhood Redevelopment Agency. She is chair of CNU's Community and Social Equity Task Force.

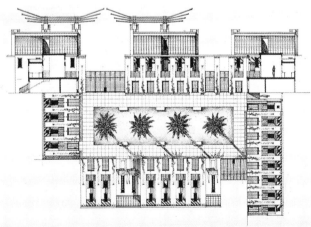

IN SOUTH CENTRAL LOS ANGELES, Vermont Village Plaza is a new mixed-use development that includes 36 affordable townhouses. Located amid a blighted three-mile strip, the project builds upon the stability of a well-kept neighborhood just a few blocks away.

Seven

Cities and towns should bring into proximity a broad spectrum of public and private uses to support a regional economy that benefits people of all incomes. Affordable housing should be distributed throughout the region to match job opportunities and to avoid concentrations of poverty.

HENRY R. RICHMOND

America faces two critical housing affordability issues: housing for urban minorities and housing for the working poor. Both are closely related to this principle's goal to break the link between inner-city disinvestment and sprawl. As I will explain, meeting this goal also can encourage the proliferation of compact, transit-oriented development.

The first critical issue to address is the provision of housing to end the social isolation of poor urban minorities. It took 100 years to end slavery in 1865. It took another 100 years to end segregation sanctioned by law. We are three decades into America's third great challenge of racial justice: to create housing policies that will enable urban minorities to live in areas of metropolitan regions where jobs are grown, schools are succeeding, and streets are safe. Affording such residential opportunities is a more effective, durable, and just approach than busing kids across town to school, operating van pools to get people from the inner city to suburban jobs, or building more jails and prisons to handle crime in American ghettos.

While middle-class blacks have made enormous housing gains in the past three decades, progress has been slow for the urban poor. Census data shows that in 1990 there were more black Americans living in urban neighborhoods with poverty rates of at least 40 percent than there were slaves in 1860. As Congress cuts support for welfare and housing, and as "minority" populations gradually replace Caucasians over the next

"One of the most pernicious results of sprawl has been the impact on African-Americans, Latinos, and on the nation's race relations. Urban disinvestment, white flight, and the concentration of poverty and minorities within city borders may seem like 'natural' facts of economic life—tragic but unavoidable. But in fact, the 'residential apartheid' that prevails in so many metropolitan regions derives from deliberate policy choices."

DAVID BOLLIER

How Smart Growth Can Stop Sprawl

"Any city, however small, is in fact divided into two, one the city of the poor, the other of the rich; they are at war with one another."

PLATO

four decades to form the new American majority, America must create housing opportunities that provide access to jobs, schools, and safe neighborhoods.

The reasons for doing so, however, go beyond the need to accord equal opportunity to all Americans. Breaking down the isolation and concentration of poor people of color will advance economic and environmental goals in which all Americans have a stake.

The critical second issue is creating housing for the working poor of any race. More than 5 million working households now pay more than half their household income for housing. This is the highest level since the Depression. While prospering seniors have lifted overall home ownership rates to 65 percent, a three-decade high, home ownership for young people is at a two-decade low. This is despite low unemployment, low mortgage rates, easing credit policies, and relaxed downpayment requirements. One part of this disparity in housing markets results from municipal zoning that prevents affordable housing by needlessly adding costs to housing. Another part stems from government's failure to make housing available to working families through incentives or supports to reduce rent or mortgage payments.

Not surprisingly, this problem is greatest in households where incomes have been plummeting for 25 years: those with incomes at the bottom 20 percent. The next 20 percent have also been going down, if less sharply. The next 20 percent have barely held their own. People in the bottom two quintiles are having real problems buying homes.

Three jurisdictions—one state and two counties—have succeeded in dealing with these two housing affordability problems. In each case, efforts to increase housing affordability in metropolitan regions have produced major community-wide benefits unrelated to housing. These benefits include reducing development pressure on farmland, increasing the feasibility of transit investment, and improving the climate for investment in the center of metropolitan regions.

LEAST COST HOUSING

Since the late 1970s, Oregon's statewide land-use program has helped the entire Portland region adopt zoning that creates more affordable housing. These reform policies were not seeking radical reform; just movement back toward traditional lot sizes and mixes of single-family to multi-family and attached houses. In 1978, the average size of a built single-family lot in Portland was 5,600 square feet. However, the average size of a vacant single-family lot in the region had gradually ballooned to 13,000 square feet. This was partly due to municipalities seeking to attract larger, more valuable housing as a tactic to increase their tax base. With land typically making up 25 percent of the cost of a house, lot size is important for affordability.

Oregon's statewide land-use policy for affordable housing requires cities to revise their zoning to reflect two trends: two decades of flat or falling household income for half the population, and fewer people per household. Between 1978 and 1983, in the 24 cities within the Portland region's Urban Growth Boundary (UGB), the average

TOO OFTEN, "AFFORDABLE" HOUSING stigmatizes its residents by looking jarringly different from the rest of the neighborhood. Here are four examples of affordable single-family and multi-family housing that negate this stigma through high-quality design.

single-family lot size was brought back down to about 8,500 square feet. In addition, the amount of land zoned for multi-family housing quadrupled from 7 percent of vacant land to 28 percent. On the same base of vacant, residentially zoned land, 305,000 housing units could be built in 1983, compared to 129,000 in 1978. Adopted in 1998, Portland Metro's 2040 plan for regional growth brought the average single-family lot even closer to "normal," to about 6,500 square feet. Thus, the Portland region has become a very efficient producer of lots inside the UGB.

These numbers show why the urban growth boundary that has enclosed this "upzoning" process since 1979 is a pro-development concept. It has made possible a nationally unprecedented, metropolitan-wide deregulation of the housing market. The higher-density zoning that resulted has benefitted many interests. The new market-sensitive zoning increased both affordability for consumers and profitability for developers. It also reduced development pressure on the urban fringe. More fundamentally, the urban growth boundary says to Oregon builders and home buyers, "We're going to reduce the cost-boosting interference in residential markets caused by local zoning." No leader of any interest group in the region wants to go back to the "good old days."

"A February 1999 report by the U.S. Conference of Mayors found that 49 percent of all households in the nation's cities owned their homes, compared to 71.5 percent in the suburbs. The U.S. mayors said that mortgage lending discrimination forces many urban home seekers to move to the suburbs to pursue the dream of home ownership."

DAVID BOLLIER
How Smart Growth Can Stop Sprawl

HOUSING AFFORDABILITY ACHIEVED BY LINKS TO TRANSIT

When launched in 1979, the Silicon Valley Manufacturing Group (SVMG) did not seem to have a land-use agenda. Yet no local organization in America has brought about more innovative and important land-use reforms. Its successes demonstrate how local groups can contain and repair sprawl while emphasizing affordable housing.

SVMG launched this effort by documenting how government policy — in this case, municipal zoning and taxation — was generating sprawl. SVMG asked the 15 municipalities in Santa Clara County for their inventories of vacant land — how much land was zoned for what class of use, at what densities, and where. SVMG was surprised that only a few cities possessed such data — let alone had mapped it. So SVMG recruited volunteers from its members and did the work itself. They found shortages and surpluses caused by policies. For example, the most optimistic industry projections foresaw 182,000 new jobs by 2010. However, municipalities desperate for tax base had zoned enough "industrial" land for 391,000 jobs. Conversely, with housing costs already affordable for only a tiny percentage of SVMG's 225,000 employees in the county, and with 108,000 new households expected to form by 2010, cities had zoned enough land to create only 69,000 homes.

SVMG then made a strategic decision to ground its alternative-to-sprawl vision in market reality. SVMG hired a survey firm to learn its employees' preferences for housing and transportation. They found 49 percent were "very or somewhat" interested in smaller or attached houses and that 65 percent would take rail transit to commute. But only 14 percent lived within a mile of the county's 21 miles of rail line. Current zoning made these choices impossible.

Given the nature of the problem and the market preferences, SVMG recommended both deregulation and new investments. These measures attracted broad support because they advanced corporate, employee, and environmental goals. For example, SVMG proposed rezoning industrial land to allow medium-density (not high-density), mixed-use, and transit-oriented new development; and argued for construction of new rail lines next to new sites for affordable housing.

With the support of conservation and community groups, critical decisions made from 1995 to 1997 helped achieve SVMG's goals. The city of San Jose adopted an urban growth boundary. Other cities are rezoning industrial land for affordable, transit-oriented housing. And voters approved a county-wide, half-cent sales tax to raise $1.8 billion to finance 77 miles of new light rail.

More than any other factor, these reforms were due to SVMG's leadership and in particular its superb 1995 report, *Creating Quality Neighborhoods: Housing Solutions for Silicon Valley*, which makes it clear that California's technology businesses depend upon sound land-use planning.

SUBSIDIZED HOUSING

Least-cost zoning, transit-oriented zoning, and transit investments can produce significant housing affordability. However, many people who wish to work near job-rich communities still cannot afford housing. This is where subsidies must play a role in the creation of scatter-site housing, or the dispersal of affordable housing throughout a community.

Some say racial tensions are too great for scatter-site housing programs to be politically realistic. Wealthy whites, the argument goes, will object to proposals to build housing designed to allow poorer people from other races to become their neighbors. Yet the nation's most successful subsidized housing program is in Maryland's Montgomery County, a well-to-do, predominantly white, Washington, D.C. suburb of 750,000. Montgomery County's housing program has proved successful over two decades, even though the county's minority population increased, and even though the county's program targeted minorities.

Since 1970, housing projects in Montgomery County with more than 50 units have been required to provide 15 percent of their units as low-income and moderately affordable. As of 1998, more than 10,000 units were built throughout the county. Of those, two-thirds were sold and one-third were rented. From 1980 to 1991, the average sale price for an affordable unit was $69,900, compared to the county average of about $208,000. More than 60 percent of the buyers of affordable units were minority members whose household

"The world we have created today as a result of our thinking thus far has problems which cannot be solved by thinking the way we thought when we created them."
ALBERT EINSTEIN

incomes were $26,400, compared to the county average of $62,000.

The program succeeds because it includes bonuses as well as mandates. Instead of assigning quotas, the county set up a builder-driven, market-friendly process. The builder says, "The county will give me a density bonus that will allow me to add about 22 percent more units to my project, because I've included 15 percent affordable and low-income units in my project. Where can I do that? Where is this going to fly?" The developer pencils it out. Except for the support from the county, the scattering of affordable, subsidized housing in Montgomery County is essentially market-driven.

Montgomery County's scatter-site housing program benefits everyone in the county, not just the people in the new houses. First, avoiding concentrations of poverty helps attain educational goals for the poor by providing new opportunities. For example, the drop-out rate in Montgomery County's schools is only 2 percent a year—one-third the national average, and one-sixth the center-city average.

In addition, deconcentrating poverty—that is, enabling the tiny percentage of poorer, minority households county-wide to live among the vast extent of middle-class neighborhoods—helps save the county's farmland. Why? Because concentrations

of poverty repel private investment from the inner city and inner suburbs. Such concentrations are thus one of the most powerful forces pushing new development out from the centers of regions. Reducing this anti-investment force—by creating opportunities for housing in all parts of the region—reduces pressure for sprawl at the edge and helps restore investment feasibility at the center.

What if all of America had used Montgomery County's technique for the last 20 years? Private developers in the U.S. build about 1.5 million housing units a year. Add to that 1.5 million the 50,000 units built by nonprofits, community development corporations, and the public housing authorities. If Montgomery County's policies had been used, America would have created about 5 million affordable housing units in 20 years, an amount equal to the 5 million households now paying more than half their income for housing.

These successes in Oregon, Silicon Valley, and Montgomery County demonstrate that the principles of New Urbanism can effectively address the nation's most daunting social problems. Focusing on a regional perspective, relaxing outmoded zoning restrictions, and investing in transit and UGBs ensures that choice-giving development patterns have a chance. The CNU Charter provides a valuable guide to all American citizens concerned with metropolitan land-use reform.

HENRY R. RICHMOND
A former board member of the CNU, Henry R. Richmond founded 1000 Friends of Oregon in the 1970s and was its executive director through 1993. In 1989 he founded the National Growth Management Leadership Project, a coalition of organizations from 24 states. He is now the executive director of the American Land Institute in Portland, Oregon.

Eight

The physical organization of the region should be supported by a framework of transportation alternatives. Transit, pedestrian, and bicycle systems should maximize access and mobility throughout the region while reducing dependence on the automobile.

G. B. ARRINGTON

The New Urbanism is not anti-car. It's about civilizing our transportation systems. It's about rewarding the typical trip—which is a short trip—by offering choices for getting around. Streets need to be designed to respect and reinforce communities. We need fewer big highways isolating and surrounding our communities, and more small roads to provide an interconnected pattern of streets and sidewalks within our communities.

We frequently look to Europe for inspiration on how to make public transit work in America. In fact, Europeans use transit only a bit more than Americans. What they do a lot more of every day is walk. By making our regions more walkable, we will take a huge step toward making them more livable, drivable, and friendly to bicycles and pedestrians.

Making this transition is challenging because the process of designing and funding our transportation system is backwards. It's a relic of the interstate system that needs to be changed. Transportation planning today rewards long trips by directing most funding to large roads linking separate communities. Yet most trips occur within a single community. The average trip in the Portland, Oregon, region, for example, is less than six miles long. Building a highway transportation system based on long trips ignores the reality of how people travel and exacerbates sprawl and congestion. It also diverts money from the inexpensive solutions, such as adequate sidewalks and street crossings, that make local trips convenient, safe, and pleasant.

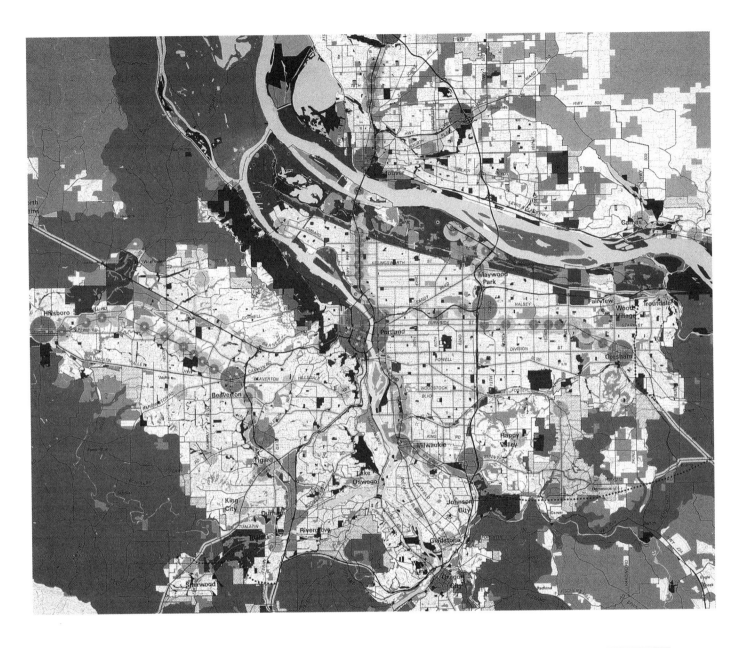

PORTLAND'S REGIONAL 2040 GROWTH CONCEPT (above) aims to increase
walk, bike, and transit trips in the region by maintaining a tight urban growth boundary
and focusing new jobs and housing near transit.

   Every transit trip begins with a walk, so safe, inviting connections between the
neighborhood and the train platform are essential. The pedestrian esplanade (right
and next page) at Gresham Central, a 90-unit infill project on Portland's MAX
light-rail line, provides just this sort of appealing link.

Reaching solutions requires basic changes in how we plan for and finance transportation. We dedicate more transportation funding to big roads because they seem to carry the most traffic. In fact, our network of small roads, if you add up all the traffic, carries more cars than the big interstates. Short trips make up most total travel each day. If we paid attention to where people want to go instead of what is easy to count, we would shift our attention and our transportation resources to the short trip.

For centuries the short trip dictated how cities were organized and developed. We have only moved away from this model in the past 50 years. Short trips remain the mother's milk of healthy communities. Places where kids bike to school, neighbors walk to the local store, and everyone carpools to soccer practice are places that work.

The roads we build have a huge effect on how much we travel. People who live in areas that contain a tight grid of streets and a mixture of land uses walk more, use transit more, and take half as many automobile trips compared to those who live in typical outer-edge suburbs. Interestingly, the more urban group drives less, but they take more total trips, including lots of short walks.

There is no transportation rule that says you have to sacrifice the community to serve it. In the past quarter-century, Portland has overhauled its transportation network to offer abundant choices for getting around—walking, biking, transit, and yes, driving. Owing to its small-block street grid, the city of Portland actually has more streets per square mile than its suburban neighbors. Places like Portland emphasize small-scale solutions—improving sidewalks to encourage the pedestrian, calming traffic to return control to neighborhoods and business districts, revising transit priorities to give buses an advantage over the car, and connecting streets so more of them lead to places rather than dead ends. In other words, we should design the road system to serve a variety of needs: to move people; to encourage compact, transit-oriented development on adjacent land; and to serve pedestrians, bikes, transit, and cars.

The suburban landscape is hostile to mobility by any mode, including the automobile. The reason is that our streets provide so few connections, and large roads divide places that should be an easy stroll apart. That's why we have mind-numbing congestion in the suburbs. Maximizing choice and mobility in our communities starts with the pedestrian, because every transit trip begins and ends with walking. Environments that serve pedestrians also work for transit. The most successful transit stops are surrounded not by parking lots but by housing and businesses within walking distance. However, planning for a viable transit system is not a prerequisite for changing the layout of our communities to make them more walkable. People in every community walk. We can begin transforming our communities in increments. One place to start would be around schools, where improvements to sidewalks and crossings would allow many more children to walk. This would make the school environment safer by reducing traffic and also

Since adopting a regional urban growth boundary in 1979, Portland's population has grown by 17 percent, but the urbanized land area of the region has expanded by less than 7 percent.

From 1995 to 1997, one of every four homes built in the Portland region was built through redevelopment and infill. During the same period, the city of Portland led the region's cities in housing starts.

Public transit is not the transportation of last choice in Portland. More than 70 percent of the region's transit riders have a car available for the trip.

Unlike any other metropolitan area in America, Portland's transit ridership is growing faster than the rate of expansion in service, population growth, or vehicle miles traveled.

THE PROCESS OF TRANSFORMING TRANSPORTATION requires tackling land use and transportation in new ways. The Round is a $100 million, mixed-use project being built on the site of a former wastewater treatment plant. Portland's MAX line runs right through the center of the site.

"Ask for the ancient paths
where the good way is;
and walk in it and find
rest for your souls."
JEREMIAH 6:16

begin to alleviate the parental burden of driving children everywhere.

While communities should focus more transportation dollars on small-scale solutions, transit agencies must completely transform their image. America is not getting on the bus. Transit is losing its share while offering a product that has changed very little in 40 years. It is not enough for transit proponents to point fingers at suburban sprawl. We can't ask transit to be the metaphorical bridge to the 21st century while riding a system locked in the past. Transit needs to appeal both to its existing market and to new markets. That means re-orienting the focus of our transit systems to serve travel within the suburbs as well as to the central city.

For transit to appeal to people in the vast majority of places in America where growth is occurring, it should include bus service that people find just as enticing as rail. Buses need to be faster, more frequent, more reliable, safer, and more comfortable using existing technology. For example, technology already can provide traffic signals to speed the bus trip by turning the signal green by remote control. Bus transit centers should be as comfortable as the best rail stations. Printed schedules must be widely and conveniently available. Low-floor buses with high windows offer a better ride. Small neighborhood buses create transit solutions appropriate to the scale of the neighborhood. A new technology provides real-time information at bus stops that informs riders when the next bus will arrive.

We can begin transforming transportation by funding more small streets, more connections, and different, not simply more, transit. But the transportation formula for livable, vibrant communities begins by rewarding the short trip and the pedestrian.

MANY PEDESTRIANS ARE IN A HOSTILE ENVIRONMENT (left). We need fewer big highways isolating and surrounding our communities, and more small roads to provide an interconnected pattern of streets and sidewalks within our communities.

G.B. ARRINGTON

G. B. Arrington is director of strategic planning for Tri-Met, Portland's transit operator, and the chair of CNU's Transportation Task Force. For more than 20 years, he has played a key role in the Portland region's experiment to reinvent the livable community by uniting transportation and land use.

Connecting Walkable Communities to Good Health

We may now be paying for building decades of auto-centered communities that discourage active lifestyles and encourage sedentary lifestyles. That price is a dramatic increase in overweight adults and children, as well as a huge number of health problems that stem from inactivity.

At an early age, we teach children that you need a car to get around. Is the car the issue or is it the way that we design our communities? We design them to move vehicles efficiently, not people— whether pedestrian or bicycle. People are viewed as hindrances.

Research suggests that, if provided with improved sidewalks and bikeways, and better connections for walking and cycling, people will indeed walk or bike more often. This shift would also reduce traffic congestion and improve air quality, and it could reduce pedestrian injuries and fatalities. A three-pronged attack on sedentary lifestyles, air quality, and pedestrian injuries could significantly improve public health.

Physical activity is the most natural behavior of humans. Until recent decades, it was a necessary part of survival. But with the advancement of industry and technology, humans have engineered the most basic form of behavior out of their lives. Recent evidence shows that the risks of a sedentary lifestyle are alarming. Sedentary lifestyles in the U.S. may be a primary factor in 200,000 deaths caused by heart disease, cancer, and diabetes each year.

Developments that emphasize mixed land use, high density, street connectivity, and pedestrian environments have a positive effect on walking and bicycling as travel choices. People would register significant benefits if they took two 15-minute walking or bicycle trips on most days of the week. In this respect, the built environment and how we travel play an important role in promoting health.

—RICHARD E. KILLINGSWORTH
AND TOM SCHMID
Centers for Disease Control and Prevention

Nine

Revenues and resources can be shared more cooperatively among the municipalities and centers within regions to avoid destructive competition for tax base and to promote rational coordination of transportation, recreation, public services, housing, and community institutions.

MYRON ORFIELD

In many regions throughout the United States, the link between local property wealth and the public services it can support leads to socioeconomic polarization among communities and sprawling, inefficient land use. Property tax-base sharing severs this detrimental link by equalizing funding for public services. It resolves the mismatch between growing social needs and shrinking property tax-based resources. Sharing property taxes undermines local fiscal incentives that support exclusive zoning and sprawl, and decreases incentives for competition for tax base among communities within a metropolitan region. It also makes regional land-use policies possible.

New Urbanists believe that public funding to support basic public services—including police and firefighters, local roads and sewers, parks, and especially local schools—should be equal throughout a metropolitan area. People of modest means shouldn't have inferior public services because they can't afford to live in property-rich communities.

School spending in particular illustrates the need for equity. About half the states have attempted to achieve equity in school funding. In Minnesota's school equity system, for example, the state provides an equal base amount of funding for each student, which may be supplemented by local districts. But even with this system, the northern, tax-base poor suburbs of the Twin Cities are still prone to high dropout rates and low college attendance. This probably results from the combination of less local voluntary

CHANGE IN
PROPERTY VALUE PER HOUSEHOLD
1980–1994

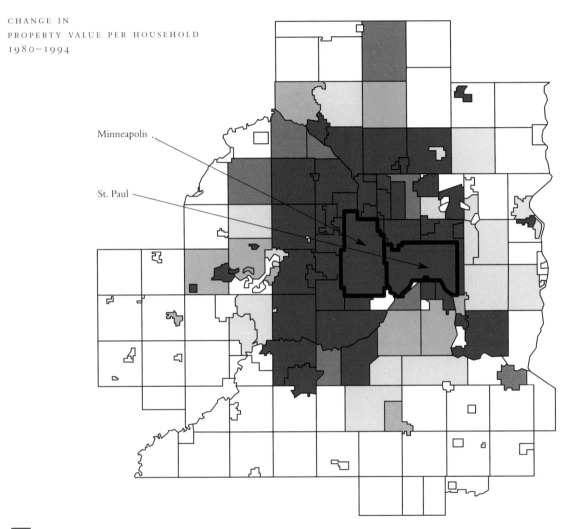

Minneapolis

St. Paul

■ Less than 10%

■ 10% to 20%

■ 20% to 30%

□ Greater than 30%

□ Excluded from survey

IN THE MINNEAPOLIS–ST. PAUL METROPOLITAN REGION, increases in property values in the outer suburbs have been outstripping those of the inner city and inner suburbs. In part this results from "exclusive" zoning in the outer suburbs. Sometimes called fiscal zoning, this system virtually requires developers to build luxury housing on large lots, and excludes the possibility of dense development or affordable housing being built in these areas.

funding and the increasing challenges of single parentage and poverty. The need for equity is especially critical in the central cities, where local tax bases are evaporating, and state and federal support for urban programs is declining.

In almost every part of the United States, wherever social needs are growing, the tax base is uncertain or declining; wherever the tax base is solid, social needs are stable or declining. In the early 1990s, for example, St. Paul had to raise taxes dramatically, but as a result of rapidly increasing social responsibilities, it also had to cut services. At the same time, dramatic tax-base increases allowed exclusive suburbs like Minnetonka and Plymouth, with their small and even declining social needs, to reduce taxes and maintain high service levels. Regionalizing the tax base would make public funds based on property wealth available for growing social needs throughout the Twin Cities region.

Currently, however, any community that can increase its tax base and limit its local social responsibilities and costs by exclusive zoning will do so. On a metropolitan level, the great disparities in tax base per household explain local fiscal incentives for exclusionary zoning. Developing communities, for example, may decide to build only houses priced above $150,000 that "pay their way." Because requiring large lots is one of the only ways to ensure that expensive houses will be built, low-density development becomes an intrinsic part of this "fiscal zoning." Regional sharing of taxes on expensive homes, however, would weaken incentives to create exclusive housing markets, and thus would limit the tendency toward large-lot sprawl.

Besides promoting low-density development patterns, a fragmented metropolitan tax base fosters unnecessary movement outward from the city. This occurs when more new housing is built on the metropolitan fringe than new households are formed in the region, and housing vacancies accumulate at the core. Both the push of decline and fiscal crisis in the urban core community, and the pull of rapidly growing communities that need tax base to pay for infrastructure, fuel this type of sprawl, as new households choose to locate in relatively problem-free communities.

In the Twin Cities, the exodus from Brooklyn Center, a declining inner suburb, to Maple Grove, a growing, exclusively residential suburb, typifies these trends. People and businesses pushed out of fiscally strapped Brooklyn Center are pulled into Maple Grove on a fiscally fueled housing boom. As Brooklyn Center declines, the number of poor children in its schools increases, crime grows, and residential property values become increasingly uncertain.

As the push of these factors gains momentum, residents move into Maple Grove and other northwestern developing suburbs. The Brookdale shopping center, an important part of Brooklyn Center's commercial-industrial base, is also in financial trouble. With deteriorating demographics, the shopping center is losing tenants and customers to a new mall in Maple Grove. At the same time, the Brookdale shopping center is becoming a popular hangout for poor youth. Brooklyn Center thus must face multiplying social needs with a crippled tax base and a highly public symbol of decline. The

"It's no longer the 'enviro crazies' who are questioning sprawl. It's God-fearing, red-meat–eating, conservative Republican county executives and town supervisors who are saying, 'Wait a minute. We can't afford this anymore.'"
ROBERT YARO

New middle-income households in the outer suburbs are imposing net public costs of between $900 and $1,500 annually, while similar households in the central city make a net contribution of between $600 and $800 a year. "Thus, locating a household in the suburbs as opposed to the central city consequently costs society on net between $1,500 and $2,300 per year."
DAVID BOLLIER
How Smart Growth Can Stop Sprawl

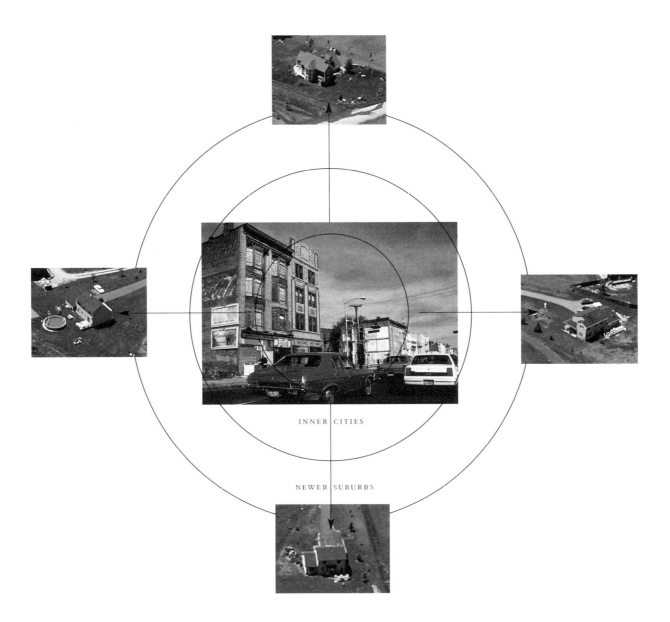

INNER CITIES

NEWER SUBURBS

SOCIOECONOMIC DECLINE MOVES OUT IN WAVES FROM THE CENTER.
Poverty and the decline of central cities roll outward to older suburbs, which are
becoming tomorrow's ghettos. Tides of middle-class homeowners sweep into communities located on the outer fringe of the metropolis. While the core areas lose the
tax base needed to pay for social services, the upper-income outer suburbs capture a
disproportionate share of economic growth and of spending on regional infrastructure.

community will have to raise taxes or cut services at the very time good services are most needed to shore up the city.

As new communities develop, they take on large debts for the concentrated development of streets, sewers, parks, and schools. Tremendous pressure builds on these local governments when debt falls due, and property tax increases seem inevitable, so they tend to spread their costs by continuing to grow. This is how tax-base fragmentation encourages low-density sprawl.

Low-density sprawl also is encouraged by building communities at densities that can't be served by public transit and with infrastructure costs that the existing tax base can't sustain. The same local fiscal pressures that encourage low-density development to enrich the tax base contribute to unnecessary low-density sprawl.

Intra-metropolitan competition for tax base harms the entire region. When cities engage in bidding wars for businesses that have already chosen to locate in a region, public moneys are used to improve one community's fiscal position and services at the expense of another's. Businesses can take advantage of this competition to shed social responsibilities. By threatening to leave, they can force troubled communities to pay them to stay. The widespread use of tax-increment financing (TIF)—which allows cities to compete (some would say gamble) for tax base, not only with their own resources but with those of the local school district, county, and state without the input of these jurisdictions—has reinforced this trend.

According to many economists, such intra-metropolitan competition damages the economic health of the whole region. As trade barriers recede, and the force of national economies fades, metropolitan areas become the basic units of global competition. Suddenly, fragmented groups of cities, fighting among themselves for government resources and economic development, are thrown into vigorous world competition against the powerful metropolitan systems of Western Europe and Asia (where expenditures for transportation, telecommunications, and education are coordinated to all jurisdictions' economic advantage).

Tax-base sharing eases the fiscal crisis in declining communities, allowing them to shore up decline. It also relieves pressure on growing communities to spread local debt costs through growth and erodes fiscal incentives encouraging low-density sprawl. As the local property tax base becomes less dependent on growth, communities can exercise a regional perspective on land use. They are able to consider measures that will benefit the region as a whole, such as urban growth boundaries, mixed-use development, greater density, and more efficient use of regional infrastructure.

"The effect of our current system of taxing buildings is one of the prime causes of our affordable housing crisis. Because it rewards decay and punishes new, high-quality construction close to the center, almost no new middle-class housing has been built since early in the 20th century. Also, under the current system, high taxes on buildings tend to be shifted to renters. This is precisely what caused the perverse conditions at the end of World War II in which the rent for Ralph Kramden's apartment was higher than the monthly mortgage payment of a house in Levittown, leading ultimately to the complete abandonment of the city by the middle class."
JAMES HOWARD
KUNSTLER
Home From Nowhere

MYRON ORFIELD

Myron Orfield is the Representative for District 60B in the Minnesota State Legislature. He is an attorney and the executive director of the Metropolitan Area Research Corporation, a Minneapolis-based organization that works with 27 metropolitan regions. Orfield is the author of *Metropolitics: A Regional Agenda for Community and Stability* (Brookings Institute / Lincoln Institute of Land Policy, 1997).

NEIGHBORHOOD, DISTRICT, AND CORRIDOR

The middle scale of the Charter is the Neighborhood, the District, and the Corridor. New Urbanism at the neighborhood scale updates timeless principles in response to new challenges. These include introducing urbanism to the suburbs, both in building and rebuilding, while respecting the fabric of communities built before World War II. Another challenge is to resolve the conflict between the fine detail of traditional urban environments and the large-scale realities of contemporary institutions and technologies. This is the heart of New Urbanism: the reassertion of fundamental urban design principles at the neighborhood scale and their unique accommodation to the contemporary world.

This section also describes an ideal structure for towns and cities. As opposed to the destructive single-use zoning of most contemporary city plans, the New Urbanism proposes a structure of three fundamental elements — neighborhoods, districts, and corridors. Viewing a community as the integration of mixed-use places rather than isolated land uses is

a profound change. It provides a planning superstructure that respects
human scale and community while creating places for larger institutions
and infrastructure. New Urbanism does not sidestep the large scale of
modern business and retailing; it simply calls for their placement
within special districts when they might overwhelm neighborhoods.

In complementary essays, Jonathan Barnett and Elizabeth
Plater-Zyberk define the need to design regions as aggregations of
neighborhoods, districts, and corridors. Walter Kulash describes
remedies to organize transportation systems in a world of sprawling
arterial roads. Marc Weiss introduces HOPE VI, the federal housing
program (devised with substantial influence from CNU members) that
has begun to replace dysfunctional housing projects with mixed-use,
mixed-income neighborhoods. The highway-fighting mayor of
Milwaukee, John Norquist, argues that traditional boulevards and
neighborhood streets add value to cities while freeways subtract from
them. William Lieberman elaborates on the connection between public
transit and dense, pedestrian-oriented neighborhoods, while Elizabeth
Moule takes a stand against auto-oriented sprawl in part because of its
negative effects on society's most disenfranchised — the poor, seniors,
women, and children. Bill Lennertz charts the connection between
thoughtful graphic design codes and mixed-use neighborhoods that
achieve and maintain their economic value. Finally, Thomas Comitta
recalls how his urban childhood in Pennsylvania was enriched by parks,
natural areas, and playing fields — and posits how this balance can be
restored between neighborhoods and their open spaces.

Ten

The neighborhood, the district, and the corridor are the essential elements of development and redevelopment in the metropolis. They form identifiable areas that encourage citizens to take responsibility for their maintenance and evolution.

JONATHAN BARNETT

THE NEIGHBORHOOD

From the study window of my house in Washington, D.C., I can see the elementary school and schoolyard diagonally across the street. Around me are houses of all shapes and sizes: some modest bungalows, a street of rowhouses opposite the school, a mix of bigger two-story dwellings, and—up the hill—some large and expensive new houses.

Two blocks away on the boulevard, there is a little shopping district with a pizza place, a video-rental store, several dry-cleaners and beauty shops, a branch post office, and a newly opened Starbucks. There are two relatively recent four-story office buildings on the boulevard with shops on their ground floors, two small apartment houses, plus a mix of one- and two-story retail buildings, some with apartments or offices upstairs. Down the hill past the boulevard there are more houses and a community park and recreation center.

Older cities and suburbs are full of neighborhoods like this. Although they continue to be good places to live, these types of neighborhoods have almost disappeared from areas planned after World War II. Instead, most recent urban and suburban developments are separate tracts of similar houses on similarly sized lots, or groups of apartment towers or garden apartments. Cars are needed for all transportation, as there are few shops, jobs, schools, or civic buildings within walking distance of homes, and densities are too low to support public transportation.

In other words, these newer areas have been planned only as single-use zoning districts: with hundreds, and sometimes thousands, of acres all zoned for the same-sized house, with occasional pockets of apartments, physically separated from single-use corridors of commercial development that is permitted only in narrow strips along major highways.

In 1929, planner Clarence Perry proposed an influential theory of neighborhood design as part of the New York City Regional Plan. Perry based the size of an ideal neighborhood on the number of families needed to support an elementary school. He also drew a circle, representing the area covered within a five-minute walking distance of a central point, over his diagrammatic plan of the neighborhood—a statement that being able to walk where you want to go remains important even when modern transportation is available.

The New Urbanism reaffirms the neighborhood as the basic building block of all residential districts. Within the 10-minute walking circle, a neighborhood includes a mix of different house and apartment types. Streets make legible connections that are easy to walk as well as drive, and there are neighborhood shops, schools, and civic buildings, all within walking distance.

"Trend is not destiny."
LEWIS MUMFORD

THE DISTRICT

While cities have always had identifiable functional districts, the practice of using laws to divide cities into districts for separate uses dates from the introduction of zoning in Germany and the Netherlands around the turn of the 20th century. Zoning is now accepted as an essential element of land-use regulation almost everywhere. There continues to be agreement that most industries require a separate district. At the other end of the land-use spectrum, large parks need to be adjacent to other activities but separated from them. However, most business and residential districts require more of a mix of uses and building types than zoning usually permits.

The New Urbanism proposes a return to the districts that include a variety of uses in addition to their primary activities. For example, all residential districts should be made up of neighborhoods.

All business districts should include a mix of shopping, offices, and residences. Mizner Park is an excellent example: a mixed-use residential, office, and business district (designed by Cooper Carry, Inc.) created on the site of a failed shopping mall in downtown Boca Raton, Florida.

FROM SINGLE-USE TO MULTI-USE DISTRICT. In Boca Raton, Florida,
a failed shopping mall was converted into a mixed-use district including residences,
offices, and shops designed around a central esplanade. Mizner Park is now one of
the most successful regional shopping districts in the country.

DUANY PLATER-ZYBERK'S
STANDARDS FOR A NEW
NEIGHBORHOOD are based
upon Clarence Perry's 1929
diagrams, describing walkable
neighborhoods such as Forest
Hills, New York, and Radburn,
New Jersey. The original
diagrams for Radburn appear
on page 80.

THE CORRIDOR

Although traditional towns and villages might have
a linear Main Street, urbanized development in
regional corridors is essentially the result of modern
transportation. Street railways produced the first
continuous neighborhoods and suburbs because the
streetcar stopped so frequently as it radiated from
the center of the city.

Recognizing in the late 1920s that the introduction of the automobile threatened to disrupt
desirable city-design patterns, Benton MacKaye and
Lewis Mumford advocated "Townless Highways"

that would connect cities and towns through non-
urbanized highway corridors, which would function
much the same way as railway lines. The purpose
of the Townless Highways was to connect two
places, not to serve as an impetus for development
between them.

A few landscaped Townless Highways were
built, notably the Merritt Parkway in Fairfield
County, Connecticut. And the interstate highway
system does not permit direct access except at
interchanges. But, in general, the timely warning of
MacKaye and Mumford was not heeded. Instead,

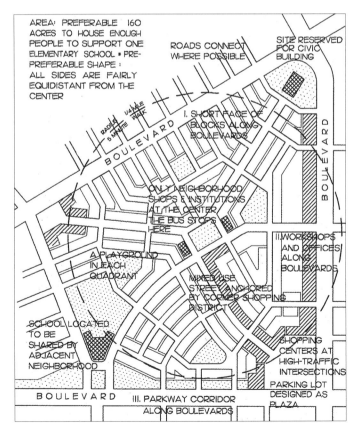

DUANY PLATER-ZYBERK'S DIAGRAM OF AN
URBAN NEIGHBORHOOD

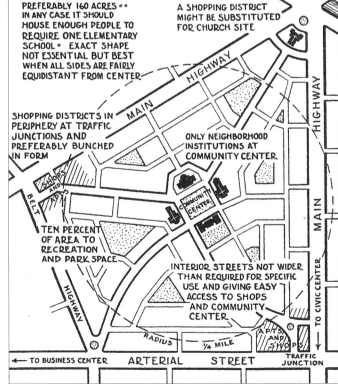

PERRY'S PLAN FOR A NEW NEIGHBORHOOD

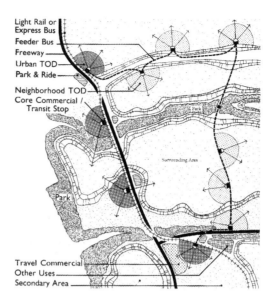

Light Rail or
Express Bus
Feeder Bus
Freeway
Urban TOD
Park & Ride
Neighborhood TOD
Core Commercial /
Transit Stop

Surrounding Area

Park

Park

Travel Commercial
Other Uses
Secondary Area

ONE ALTERNATIVE to sprawling strip development involves creating nodes of transit-oriented development at one-mile intervals along a corridor.

continuous commercial strips—zoning districts originally devised for frontages along streetcar streets—were zoned along arterials and highways in suburbs and rural areas.

This practice proved a planning disaster. The commercial strip provides far too much land zoned for business to create any incentive to use it efficiently, while there is not enough appropriately zoned land at any one location to create anything like a town or city center.

Land in urbanized corridors along highways can be developed in districts dense enough to be served by public transit as well as automobiles. Residential and industrial districts can be related to each other, and residential, industrial, and business districts can be separated by rural and low-density suburban areas. Existing commercial strips can be made into more intensive districts at appropriate locations.

Modern transportation also makes it both necessary and possible to designate regional parks as corridors. Benton MacKaye first proposed a protected Appalachian Highlands corridor stretching from Maine to Georgia in 1921. The 2,100-mile-long Appalachian Trail is a large portion of MacKaye's concept that has since been implemented. The protection of natural systems that form regional corridors is an important element of the New Urbanism.

"The Townless Highway begets the Highwayless Town in which the needs of close and continuous human association on all levels will be uppermost.... For the highwayless town is based upon the notion of effective zoning of functions through initial public design, rather than by blind legal ordinances."
LEWIS MUMFORD
"What Is a City"
Architectural Record, 1937

JONATHAN BARNETT

CNU board member Jonathan Barnett is the principal of Jonathan Barnett, FAIA, AICP, in Washington, D.C. He is also a professor of City and Regional Planning at the University of Pennsylvania. His numerous books on urban design include Urban Design as Public Policy, Introduction to Urban Design, The Elusive City, and The Fractured Metropolis.

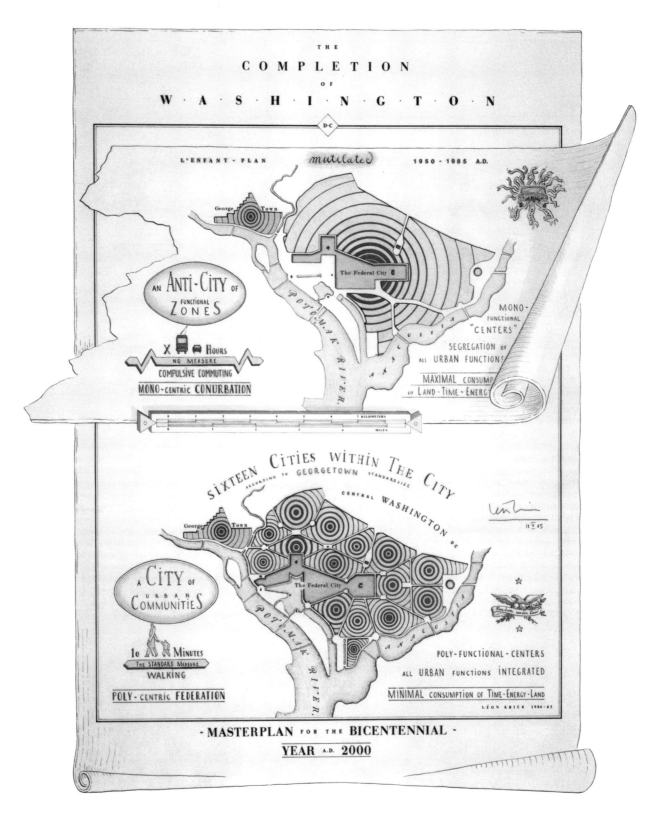

LEON KRIER'S EXPRESSIVE DIAGRAMS illustrate the difference between a zoned "anti-city" and a "poly-centric city of urban communities" based upon efficient walking distances.

Eleven

Neighborhoods should be compact, pedestrian-friendly, and mixed-use. Districts generally emphasize a special single use, and should follow the principles of neighborhood design when possible. Corridors are regional connectors of neighborhoods and districts; they range from boulevards and rail lines to rivers and parkways.

ELIZABETH PLATER-ZYBERK

The fundamental elements of a true urbanism are the neighborhood, the district, and the corridor. Neighborhoods are urbanized areas having a balanced range of human activity. Districts are urbanized areas organized around a predominant activity such as a college campus. Corridors are linear systems of transportation or green space that connect and separate the neighborhoods and districts.

THE NEIGHBORHOOD

Neighborhoods mass together to form towns and cities. A single neighborhood isolated in the landscape is a village. Though the nomenclature varies, there is general agreement regarding the composition of the neighborhood. The neighborhood unit of the 1929 New York Regional Plan, the Quarter (right) described by Leon Krier, the traditional neighborhood development (TND), and transit-oriented development (TOD) all share similar attributes. They are:

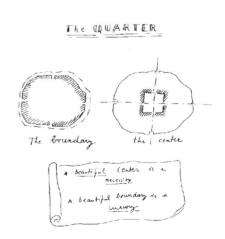

I. THE NEIGHBORHOOD HAS A CENTER AND AN EDGE.

The combination of a focus and a limit contribute to the social identity of the community. Though both are important, the center is necessary. The center is usually a public space—a square, a green, or an important street intersection. It is located near the center of the neighborhood unless geography dictates that it be located elsewhere. Eccentric locations may be justified by a shoreline, a transportation corridor, or a promontory creating a view.

"In recent decades Americans have been focusing too much on the house itself and too little on the neighborhood, too much on the interior luxury and too little on public amenity. By reconsidering the design of our houses, we might begin again to create walkable, stimulating, more affordable neighborhoods where sociable pleasures are always within reach. The country can learn much from the neighborly kinds of housing we used to build. They made—and continue to make—good places for living."

PHILIP LANGDON
A Better Place to Live

BY 1928, THERE WERE ALREADY 21.3 MILLION CARS on America's roads. Clarence Stein and Henry Wright's 1928 general plan for Radburn, New Jersey, put the pedestrian first by placing most of life's needs within a short stroll in neighborhoods for 10,000 people. Shopping centers placed at the edges are accessible both by foot and by car.

The center is the location for civic buildings, such as libraries, meeting halls, and churches. Commercial buildings including shops and workplaces are also associated with the center of a village. But in the aggregations of neighborhoods that create towns and cities, commercial buildings are often at the edge where, combined with the commercial edges of other neighborhoods, they form a town center.

The edge of a neighborhood varies in character. In villages, the edge borders the lowest density of housing and is usually defined by land reserved for cultivation or conservation in a natural state. In urban areas, the neighborhood edge is often defined by boulevards or parkways, which may be lined by higher-density buildings.

2. THE NEIGHBORHOOD HAS A BALANCED MIX OF ACTIVITIES: SHOPPING, WORK, SCHOOLING, RECREATION, AND ALL TYPES OF HOUSING.

This arrangement is particularly useful for those—young, old, handicapped, or poor—who can't depend on the automobile for mobility.

The neighborhood provides housing for a range of incomes. Affordable housing types include backyard cottages, apartments above shops, and rowhouses. Houses and apartments for the wealthy may occupy the choice sites.

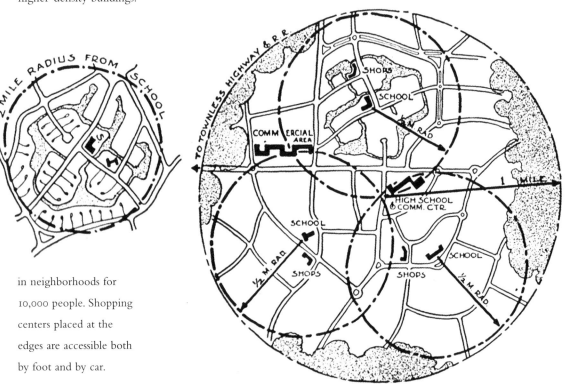

3. THE IDEAL SIZE OF A NEIGHBORHOOD IS A QUARTER-MILE FROM CENTER TO EDGE.

This distance is the equivalent of a five-minute walk at an easy pace. Within this five-minute radius, residents can walk to the center from anywhere in the neighborhood to take care of many daily needs or to use public transit. The location of a bus or light-rail stop within this walking distance substantially increases the likelihood that people will use public transit.

A cluster or string of transit-oriented neighborhoods creates a regional network of villages, towns, and cities that people can get to without relying solely on cars. Such a system provides access to major cultural and social institutions, a variety of shops, and the kind of broad job base that can be supported only by a substantial population of many neighborhoods.

4. NEIGHBORHOOD STREETS ARE DETAILED TO PROVIDE EQUALLY FOR THE PEDESTRIAN, THE BICYCLE, AND THE AUTOMOBILE.

Neighborhood streets that provide wide sidewalks, street trees, and on-street parking increase pedestrian activity. People are more apt to want to walk or bicycle if the route provides safe, pleasant, shady sidewalks and bike lanes. Drivers are more apt to drive slower in areas with pedestrian-filled sidewalks, crosswalks, and convenient, on-street parking. Streets designed for pedestrians, bicyclists, and drivers also encourage the casual meetings among neighbors that help form the bonds of community.

Neighborhood streets are laid out to create blocks for building sites and to shorten pedestrian routes. An interconnected network of streets and small blocks provides multiple driving routes that diffuse traffic and keep local traffic away from long-range transportation corridors.

5. THE NEIGHBORHOOD GIVES PRIORITY TO THE CREATION OF PUBLIC SPACE AND TO THE APPROPRIATE LOCATION OF CIVIC BUILDINGS.

Private buildings form an edge that delineates public spaces and the private block interior. Public spaces such as formal squares, informal parks, and small playgrounds provide places for gathering and recreation. Sites that honor individuals or events are reserved for public buildings such as schools, municipal buildings, and concert halls. Such sites help support the civic spirit of the community and provide places where people can gather for educational, social, cultural, and religious activities.

THE DISTRICT

The district is an urbanized area with special functions, such as a theater district, capitol area, or college campus. Other districts accommodate large-scale transportation or workplaces, such as industrial parks, airports, storage and shipping terminals, and refineries. Although districts preclude the full range of activities of a neighborhood, they need not be the single-activity zones of suburbia; complementary activities can support the district's primary identity.

"We complain that the streets of the urban peripheries are boring, that they do not offer the same opportunities for encounter, exchange, curiosity, attention, offered by the streets of the historic centers. It is not surprising, as the streets of the historic centers were made for the motion of human beings whereas the streets of the periphery have been made for the motion of automobiles."
GIANCARLO DE CARLO
The Contemporary Town

THE CITY OF WEST
SACRAMENTO. A neighbor-
hood center connected to a
town center at a transit stop.

"Above all else, a city is
a means of providing a
maximum number of social
contacts and satisfactions.
When the open spaces
gape too widely, and the
dispersal is too constant,
the people lack a stage
for their activities and the
drama of their daily life
lacks sharp focus."
LEWIS MUMFORD
The Highway and the City

The structure of the district parallels the neighborhood. It has an identifiable focus that provides orientation and identity, and clear boundaries that allow for special taxing or management organizations. Like the neighborhood, the district features public spaces—plazas, sidewalks, important intersections—that reinforce a sense of community among users, encourage pedestrians, and ensure security. Transit systems benefit districts greatly and should be connected to neighborhoods within a regional network.

THE CORRIDOR

The corridor is the connector or separator of neighborhoods and districts. Corridors are composed of natural and technical components ranging from wildlife trails to rail lines. The corridor is not the haphazardly residual "open space" buffering the enclaves of suburbia, but a deliberate civic element characterized by its continuity. It is defined by the boundaries of neighborhoods and districts and provides entry to them.

The path of a transportation corridor is determined by the intensity of its use. Highways and heavy-rail corridors remain tangential to towns and cities and enter only the industrial districts. Light rail and bus corridors may be incorporated into the boulevards at the edges of neighborhoods, where transit stops are designed for pedestrian use and can accommodate building sites. Bus corridors may pass into neighborhood centers on small conventional streets.

Transportation corridors may be laid out within continuous parkways, providing long-distance walking and bicycle trails and a continuous natural habitat. Green corridors or greenways can also be formed by natural systems such as streams, drainage ditches engineered for irrigation, or as a result of drainage systems for water runoff. These greenways may include recreational open spaces, such as parks, playing fields, schoolyards, and golf courses. Such continuous natural spaces should gradually flow to the rural edges, connecting the regional ecosystem.

ELIZABETH PLATER-ZYBERK
Elizabeth Plater-Zyberk is Dean of the University of Miami School of Architecture and a founding principal of Duany Plater-Zyberk & Company, an architecture and town planning firm in Miami that has designed numerous New Urbanist communities. She is a founding board member of CNU.

Twelve

Many activities of daily living should occur within walking distance, allowing independence to those who do not drive, especially the elderly and the young. Interconnected networks of streets should be designed to encourage walking, reduce the number and length of automobile trips, and conserve energy.

WALTER KULASH

Transportation is one of the most controversial elements in community development. In New Urbanist communities, transportation planning focuses on reducing dependence on the automobile, increasing public transit use, and developing a more flexible road system. These actions help reduce local traffic problems, conserve energy, improve air quality, and encourage people to walk, bike, or take the bus to get around within their neighborhood or district.

The street layout of a community in large part dictates the effectiveness of its transportation system. The connected street network, essential to the New Urbanism, appears in a wide variety of street patterns. The successful network can be highly regular and rectilinear, such as the grid found in many neotraditional new towns, or it can be informal and highly irregular, as in New England towns and European city cores. The connected network benefits traffic by providing a direct route between where people live and their daily destinations. This network also offers a vast number of different routes for traffic, as well as many intersections, which increase left-turn options and reduce the bottleneck congestion found in most road systems. Traffic is thus diffused over miles of streets.

Until the 1930s, highly connected street networks were built into every form of settlement in the United States. The connected street network was so fundamental to town builders' thinking that it did not need to be codified. In the 1930s, the notion

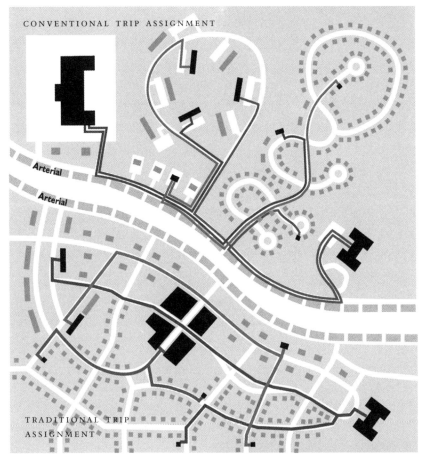

CONVENTIONAL TRIP ASSIGNMENT

Arterial

Arterial

TRADITIONAL TRIP
ASSIGNMENT

IN A TYPICAL
SUBURBAN LAYOUT (top),
even short trips are directed
to arterial roads, creating
traffic congestion. Under
traditional "trip assignment,"
local roads become more
useful for local trips.
Traffic is distributed rather
than coagulated.

that U.S. cities needed to be redesigned for the
automobile appeared, bringing concepts such as
separate arterial and collector roads whose only
purpose was to carry traffic. These principles were
codified into planning regulations during the
post–World War II suburban building boom. They
called for street systems deliberately designed to
keep through traffic off residential streets, and they
specified the antithesis of connected streets: isolated
pods of development connected only to a sparse
system of arterial highways. Street layouts were no
longer networks, but instead became "dendritic"
in nature, with all streets branching from a single
connection to the regional arterial road system.
The conventional suburban street hierarchy was
designed to consist of local streets ending in
cul-de-sacs and collector streets that collect vehicles
and feed them into major arterial streets that link
different neighborhoods and districts.

Traffic planning techniques of "assigning"
traffic—or assigning the projected quantity of
travel on specific routes, based on notions such as
how many trips a typical family might make each
day—reveal the important advantages of a highly
connected network:

- Local traffic, which comprises 70 percent of
  all vehicular traffic, stays local. With the connected street network, local traffic uses small
  local streets and never enters the major arterial
  system. By contrast, the conventional suburban
  pattern of cul-de-sacs feeding into a main
  arterial compels all drivers into the arterial

system. This focusing of all traffic onto arterial highways produces intersection congestion even in low-density developments and creates the defining characteristics of suburban sprawl-pattern traffic.

- Travel is more direct. In a network, the large number of highly connected streets ensures the shortest possible travel distance for any given trip. This short travel distance also reflects the ability to reach most destinations from all directions, thereby eliminating the need to make a circuitous trip on arterial highways.

- The highly connected network allows the arterial streets to more efficiently accommodate trips most important to the region, such as longer-distance drives to work and trips for specialty shopping and medical care. This is the mission of these roads, according to state departments of transportation, typically the arterial roads' "owner." Attempting to accommodate short, local, daily trips is an abuse of the intended function of arterial streets and fuels much of the demand for more and wider highways.

- Creating town centers. The highly connected network fosters the development of a true town center. Traffic is able to reach the town center from all directions, using numerous possible routes. The highly connected network also promotes centralized activities, whereas the conventional suburban pattern rewards the

sprawl of activities located in thin strips along major highways. (Public efforts to limit or eliminate strip development through such regulatory efforts as master plans, zoning, and site plan regulations are easily circumvented by landowners and conventional suburban developers.)

- Non-vehicular travel. The highly connected grid is an ideal environment for walking, biking, and public transit because it provides direct connections between where people live and where they need to go. Walking and biking are pleasant because of the wide variety of street environments on different routes and the low levels of traffic on the streets. The conventional suburban layout, on the other hand, is the worst possible environment for pedestrian travel. Access between peoples' homes and their destinations is seldom direct, and it usually requires travel through hostile environments such as major arterial streets and parking lots. In conventional suburban development, few if any frequent or typical trips are within walking distance—up to 1,300 feet, or up to only 500 feet through unpleasant circumstances such as parking lots. And walking or biking often is dangerous and unpleasant because there are no sidewalks, or they may exist only on the multi-lane arterial road where traffic is heavier and faster, with much greater noise and fumes.

"It is sad to see how many cities have this emptiness at their core.... What they need is pedestrian congestion. But what they are doing is taking what people are on the streets and putting them somewhere else. In a kind of holy war against the street, they are putting them up in overhead skyways, down in underground concourses, and into sealed atriums and galleries. They are putting them everywhere except at street level.

...But one can hope. I think the center is going to hold. I think it is going to hold because of the way people demonstrate by their actions how vital is centrality. The street rituals and encounters that seem so casual, the prolonged goodbyes, the 100 percent conversations—these are not at all trivial. They are manifestations of one of the most powerful of impulses: the impulse to the center.

And of the primacy of the street. It is the river of life of the city, the place where we come together, the pathway to the center."

WILLIAM H. WHYTE
City: Rediscovering the Center

Rearranging neighborhoods into a highly connected street network radically improves the pedestrian environment because all the typical daily trip destinations are within a short walk of each other. Sidewalks actually become the community's premier public space. The highly connected network also increases public transit use. Peoples' perception that their sidewalks and streets are pleasant and safe is the key factor in whether they will use public transit, because all bus and light-rail trips begin and end as walking trips.

The highly connected network supports the "park once" pattern in which drivers regard their destination as a district—downtown or a town center—rather than a single property. Although drivers use their cars to arrive at a shopping district or town center, they will park in one spot, usually in public or on-street parking, and then take a walking tour that includes all the destinations on their lists, such as places for shopping, entertainment, or business. This contrasts sharply with the pattern of travel in typical suburban layouts, where people drive to each destination and attempt to park there. Driving to additional destinations requires repeating the process, each time turning out onto a major arterial road.

Though some studies have quantified a significant reduction of vehicle miles traveled in New Urbanist communities compared to conventional suburban communities, the traffic pattern of New Urbanist communities is so superior that people do not need empirical evidence. People become convinced when they don't have to go out onto an arterial road to do their grocery shopping or take their child to school.

"Americans are in the habit of never walking if they can ride."
LOUIS PHILIPPE
Duc d'Orleans, 1798

WALTER KULASH

Walter Kulash is a principal and senior traffic engineer with Glatting Jackson Kercher Anglin Lopez Rinehart, a community planning firm in Orlando, Florida. He has been a consultant for traffic and transit planning projects throughout the United States and Canada, including local and state governments and numerous neotraditional communities.

PROPOSED REDESIGN OF PALM CANYON DRIVE in Cathedral City, California. An unsightly strip with 30,000 cars a day zooming by deteriorating buildings, Palm Canyon will be remade with extensive landscaping and sidewalks. Some 100 acres of new buildings frame public spaces. Urban design standards require inviting building entries, canopies, and lighting that encourage pedestrians.

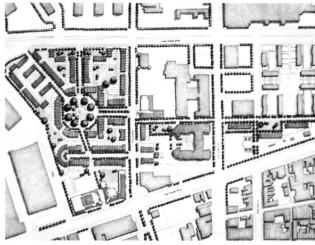

1920s   1950s   1998

FIVE BLOCKS EAST OF BALTIMORE CITY HALL, Pleasant View Gardens is the
first project completed under the federal program called HOPE VI—otherwise known
as Homeownership Opportunities for People Everywhere. Pleasant View Gardens
replaced grim 1950s-style high-rise public housing with rowhouses, senior housing,
and mixed uses. Narrow streets and small blocks typical of Baltimore's historic
neighborhoods were reinstated in place of "superblocks."

Thirteen

Within neighborhoods, a broad range of housing types and price levels can bring people of diverse ages, races, and incomes into daily interaction, strengthening the personal and civic bonds essential to an authentic community.

MARC A. WEISS

One of the greatest challenges facing the future of metropolitan America is to break up the concentration of poverty in inner-city and inner-suburban neighborhoods. Especially among minorities, particularly African-Americans and Latinos, families are increasingly isolated in communities where too few people have good-paying jobs or own thriving businesses. In these low-income neighborhoods, far too many people are unemployed, living on welfare, working part-time, or even working full-time but for such low wages that they cannot adequately support their children.

Initiatives such as Chicago's Gautreaux program, where low-income families living in inner-city, high-poverty neighborhoods are given the opportunity to move to mixed-income communities, have proven to be highly successful in expanding the availability of jobs, increasing incomes, and improving educational performance. Connecting low-income people to suburban jobs and homes is one much-needed approach; the other is rebuilding cities by bringing back working families through attractive amenities, healthy economies, and affordable homeownership.

The Clinton Administration, led by Secretary Henry Cisneros of the U.S. Department of Housing and Urban Development (HUD), took up the challenge of generating greater metropolitan diversity and investing in urban revitalization. To accomplish this, HUD drew on the expertise and vision of the Congress for the New Urbanism. I served as HUD's New Urbanism liaison, reaching out to CNU members and involving them in creating and implementing successful new national

1899   1940   1970   1999

THE TOWNHOMES ON CAPITOL HILL, a HOPE VI project, replaces 5.3 acres of
abandoned public housing in Washington, D.C., with 154 new homes, a community
building, and new public streets. Affordable and market-rate homes are designed to the
same standard. Variety is assured through 35 different facade designs, 30 window configurations, and 22 types of bricks, all based upon historical precedent on Capitol Hill.
Figure-ground diagrams show how streets deteriorated from 1899 to 1970 as vacant
lots and wide roads proliferated, and how this has been repaired.

RANDOLPH NEIGHBOR-
HOOD, a HUD-funded
neighborhood redevelop-
ment in Richmond,
Virginia (before and after).

programs and local development strategies. The basic philosophy behind our work with CNU is explained in a HUD publication, *New American Neighborhoods: Building Homeownership Zones to Revitalize Our Nation's Communities:*

"Rebuilding neighborhoods with hundreds of new homes presents an exciting opportunity to create better and more livable communities. In recent years, architects, planners, landscape designers, and developers have experimented with the principles of a New Urbanism, combining features of traditional community planning with new ways of organizing daily life in a rapidly changing world.

"The fundamental idea is to view the neighborhood as a coherent unit, where adults and children can walk to nearby shopping, services, schools, parks, recreation centers, and, in some cases, to their own jobs and businesses; where civic centers can serve as focal points for community activity; where streets and blocks are connected with pedestrian walkways and bicycle paths; where public transit is readily available to connect with other neighborhoods and communities throughout the metropolitan region; where automobiles are convenient to use but do not dominate the most visible aspects of the urban landscape with traffic congestion and massive parking lots; and where houses are built closer together, with front and back porches and yards, grouped around tree-shaded squares, small parks, and narrow streets with planting strips.

"Such pedestrian-friendly environments help facilitate positive community spirit and emphasize neighborhood safety and security. The goal of

New Urbanism is to promote diverse and livable communities with a greater variety of housing types, land uses, and building densities—in other words, to develop and maintain a melting pot of neighborhood homes serving a wide range of household and family sizes, ages, cultures, and incomes."

Our goal at HUD was to support the rebuilding of both urban and suburban neighborhoods, respectively, by promoting a mixed-income environment with greater economic and social diversity, along with a mixed-use environment that included better design, planning, and development of land and buildings. Nowhere was this change more urgently needed than in public housing. In many cities the most isolated, deteriorating, and poorest neighborhoods were "the projects." We wanted public housing to become like *Where's Waldo?*— invisible in the urban landscape, interwoven into the wider metropolitan fabric, indistinguishable from all other types of private and publicly assisted homes and apartments.

To pursue this vitally important objective, we established the HOPE VI program to radically transform public housing developments by demolishing vacant high-rise buildings and reconnecting low-income residents to their surrounding neighborhoods; attracting mixed-income populations through a combination of public and private housing, both rental and homeownership; and building genuine community through economic development, human services, and good planning and design. CNU members used considerable

"One of the unsuitable ideas behind projects is the very notion that they are projects, abstracted out of the ordinary city and set apart. To think of salvaging or improving projects, as projects, is to repeat this root mistake. The aim should be to get that project, that patch upon the city, rewoven back into the fabric—and in the process of doing so, strengthen the surrounding fabric too."

JANE JACOBS
The Death and Life of Great American Cities

IN PITTSBURGH, CRAWFORD SQUARE in the Lower Hill neighborhood was

vacant for 25 years. The redevelopment included 331 residences—rental and owner-

occupied—built around parks and reconstituted streets. The revived neighborhood

is racially mixed and equally divided between market-rate and affordable homes.

expertise in redesigning public housing developments including Diggs Town in Norfolk. They are assisting HUD and local public housing authorities in spending billions of dollars wisely on redeveloping public housing communities in Baltimore, Charlotte, Chicago, Detroit, Washington, D.C., Boston, Cleveland, Philadelphia, Pittsburgh, Atlanta, Louisville, and dozens of additional cities.

Similarly, when the Clinton Administration embarked on its ambitious Empowerment Zones and Enterprise Communities initiative and its new Homeownership Zones program, we turned to the New Urbanists for help in developing innovative concepts and methods of community planning and urban design. Secretary Cisneros asked the CNU to form an Inner City Task Force to work with HUD and local communities in applying the principles of New Urbanism to rebuild inner-city and inner-suburban neighborhoods. The CNU leadership then asked Secretary Cisneros to sign the Charter, and he did so when he gave the keynote address at the Charleston congress in 1996. Since that time, CNU's Inner City Task Force has played a major role in both the HOPE VI and Homeownership Zones efforts, serving as faculty in HUD-sponsored

courses to educate and train local officials in the use of New Urbanist ideas to improve development practices and build better communities.

Leaders of the Congress for the New Urbanism produced for HUD a landmark document, Principles for Planning and Designing Homeownership Zones, based on the key ideas in CNU's Charter. This document was used by all of the 110 local government applicants for the $100 million nationwide Homeownership Zones grants competition in 1996. HUD awarded extra points to applicants for development proposals that incorporated "innovative and creative community planning and design" strategies using New Urbanism principles.

The bottom line is this: To achieve a prosperous and just society with a high quality of life for all our citizens and families, economic, social, and physical diversity are essential elements for the long-term success of every neighborhood and community. One of the best ways to promote such a healthy diversity of homes and people is by utilizing the principles of the Charter of the New Urbanism.

"Nobody not under the control of some bureaucrat or commissar would ever wish to live in a 'housing project'... nobody not under some such control ever has."

PETER BLAKE
Form Follows Fiasco

MARC A. WEISS

Marc A. Weiss, Ph.D., a former professor of urban development and planning at Columbia University, served as special assistant to the Secretary of the U.S. Department of Housing and Urban Development (HUD) from 1993 to 1997 and was a senior policy adviser to the Clinton–Gore campaign and transition in 1991 and 1992. Weiss is a senior fellow at the Center for National Policy in Washington, D.C., and is the author of many books and articles, including *The Rise of the Community Builders* and *Real Estate Development Principles and Process.* He is currently co-authoring a book with Henry Cisneros on the future of American cities and regions.

Diggs Town, Norfolk, Virginia

The Diggs Town housing project was once a dangerous, decaying, 30-acre island of impenetrable superblocks where gunshots rang out in the night. Today, thanks to a unique collaboration between architects and tenants, it has become a genuine neighborhood, with lovingly tended yards and flower gardens, safe, well-traveled streets, and a burgeoning sense of community.

Architects began the redesign by opening up the project to the surrounding neighborhoods and transforming it into a series of small villages. New streets and paths have given it the texture of a normal neighborhood in which each unit faces a street and has its own address and front yard. Picket fences help define private and public areas, and traditional porches allow tenants to talk with neighbors while keeping an eye on the street. Drug dealers, finding little privacy in the narrow streets, have gone elsewhere, and crime and violence have decreased. And now that they are in charge of the space in front of their homes, residents have begun to care for their properties and take pride in them.

While no one believes that the physical changes in Diggs Town have solved all of its problems (65 percent of the 4,000 tenants live below the poverty line), the newly energized community has been liberated from the stigma attached to public housing.

—GIANNI LONGO
A Guide to Great American Public Places

DIGGS TOWN
TRANSFORMED:
Common areas that had
become urban DMZs
were revived by re-creating
neighborhood street patterns
lined by front porches.
Each house now provides
an individual address
for residents.

Key Elements of HOPE VI

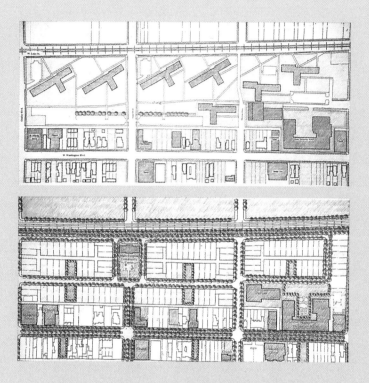

IN CHICAGO, THE HORNER NEIGHBORHOOD PLAN eliminates dysfunctional 13-story towers of public housing and replaces them with townhouses, duplexes, and small apartment buildings. Intimate, tree-lined streets supplant the inhumane, unsafe "superblocks."

- New developments are designed to human scale. Superblocks are divided into smaller blocks. High-rise buildings are demolished and replaced with townhomes, single-family homes, and smaller apartment buildings.

- Civic uses such as recreation and medical facilities, village centers, and shops and small businesses are included in the neighborhoods.

- Market-rate and affordable housing are indistinguish-able from each other.

- Resident incomes are mixed; units are rented or owned by middle-class, working-class, and publicly subsidized households.

- Homes are close to the street, with front windows and porches.

- Residents have street addresses rather than project addresses.

- Back and front yards belong to individual units, creating "defensible space."

- Parks are small and placed where they can be observed closely by residents.

- New streets that break up "superblocks" are designed to be relatively narrow and have on-street parking and traffic-calming devices like crosswalks.

- Tenants are carefully screened, and rules are strictly enforced.

MILWAUKEE'S LATE, GREAT BRONZEVILLE, a once-proud African-American
commercial hub where Duke Ellington played after hours, was removed without
a trace—replaced in 1966 by construction of Interstate 43.

Fourteen

Transit corridors, when properly planned and coordinated, can help organize metropolitan structure and revitalize urban centers. In contrast, highway corridors should not displace investment from existing centers.

JOHN O. NORQUIST

In 1941, Norman Bel Geddes, the father of the interstate highway system, warned that the revolutionary highway system he envisioned could harm cities. "A great motorway has no business cutting a wide swath right through a town or city and destroying the values there," he wrote in his book, *Magic Motorways*. "Its place is in the country."

Unfortunately, such warnings went unheeded. Instead, the federal government today funds 90 percent of the cost of freeways that cities would never build on their own. With that money, pork-barrel politicians, state bureaucrats, and highway contractors chop up cities with miles of high-priced concrete.

Even today, many of Milwaukee's residents, business owners, and municipal leaders must fight the retrograde highway lobby, which seeks to spend $1.3 billion to rebuild a multi-level interstate interchange and add lanes to Interstate 94. This expansion would stretch 13 miles from the heart of the city, siphoning life from city neighborhoods and businesses into suburban Waukesha County.

Milwaukee has been down this traumatic road before. In 1966, construction of Interstate 43 plowed right through Eighth and Walnut, the city's African-American commercial and cultural hub. Few thought twice about it. State Representative Lloyd Barbee picketed the first bulldozer in protest of what he called the "dirty ditch." But his action was futile. Once-proud Bronzeville, Milwaukee's little version of Harlem's 125th and Lenox, was removed without a trace, except for an annual remembrance in a nearby park. The Flame nightclub where Duke Ellington once played after hours, the

"If the purpose of the motorway as now conceived is that of being a high-speed, non-stop thoroughfare, the motorway would only bungle the job if it got caught up with the city.... A great motorway has no business cutting a wide swath right through a town or city and destroying the values there; its place is in the country."
NORMAN BEL GEDDES
Magic Motorways

"The right to have access to every building in the city by private motorcar, in an age when everyone possesses such a vehicle, is actually the right to destroy the city."
LEWIS MUMFORD
The Highway and the City

"The autobahns may have inspired the interregional highways, but on one element they differed fundamentally: the German roads sought to serve the cities, while the American roads aimed to change them. The variance would become startlingly apparent a generation later."
STEPHEN B. GODDARD
Getting There: The Epic Struggle between Road and Rail in the Twentieth Century

tobacco shop, and even Representative Barbee's office above a shoe repair shop are gone.

Milwaukee's Italian-American community wielded more clout than Bronzeville. The Italians operated Milwaukee's still-vibrant wholesale food district in the 1950s, when the Wisconsin Department of Transportation (WisDOT) proposed Interstate 794 through the Third Ward. Residents resisted—at least for a while. With the late 1960s construction of I-794, supporters of "progress" prevailed, but not until WisDOT and the county agreed to place a monument to the demolished Church of Our Lady of Pompeii (above), the community's former spiritual center and chief landmark. In the two years after the elevated freeway was built, the neighborhood declined so fast that the city considered turning the remains of the Third Ward into a pornographic "combat zone." This indignity was too much for even those who supported "progress," and the plan failed. Today the Third Ward prospers—except for portions next to the noise and smell of the freeway, where most buildings have crumbled or been razed for surface parking lots.

What are the lessons to be learned from these once-vibrant ethnic urban centers? One is that freeways can destroy rather than enhance property values in cities. Another is that freeways impose physical obstacles that divide neighborhood from neighborhood. This stunts what Jane Jacobs calls the "unplanned combinations of existing ideas" that occur in traditional cities, spawning innovations that build our economy.

There are many sound alternatives to freeway expansion. The most important ones involve protecting vital urban neighborhoods, while also creating a more diverse regional transit system that includes rail. Visit cities where rail transit still exists or has been expanded—Boston or San Diego, for example—and you'll find viable downtowns and lively neighborhoods. Even a low-density, auto-oriented city like Dallas has benefitted from the light-rail system known as DART—Dallas Area Rapid Transit. The 20-mile "starter" (projected to reach at least 53 miles) system has attracted daily ridership that is 20 percent beyond original estimates, while drawing more than $650 million to real-estate projects along the line. Some neighborhoods that once fought placement of stations in their areas are now clamoring for them.

Another attraction of rail is that people usually prefer trains because they are faster and more comfortable than buses. When rail transit is made available, many people will immediately switch from the private auto. Rail also creates opportunities to build or improve compact neighborhoods near transit stations. Studies conducted in Chicago, Los Angeles, and San Francisco indicate that vehicle miles traveled (VMT) decline between 14 and 30 percent for every doubling in residential density. People who live in reasonably dense communities served by transit often save money because they drive less or own fewer cars per family.

Rediscovering the traditional street pattern of avenues, boulevards, and streets creates another alternative to building freeways. Unlike freeways, whose only functions are to carry vehicles, an avenue adds value to the city. Boulevard systems in Denver and Kansas City, for example, create miles of beautifully landscaped linear parkways that anchor strong neighborhoods. Built to meet a variety of public and private needs, avenues and boulevards tend to foster stable land values. Milwaukee's Forest Home Avenue, the Bronx's Grand Concourse, Wilshire Boulevard in Los Angeles, and Chicago's Michigan Avenue continue to attract investment and experience impressive increases in property value.

The highway lobby argues that more freeways are the only solution to reduce congestion and pollution by moving vehicles faster. They say rail is old-fashioned, inflexible, and too costly, and that urban sprawl is the reality because people prefer the suburbs. Such logic ignores many facts in favor of traditional neighborhoods and street patterns served by rail. Freeways actually induce more and longer trips, while congestion and pollution get worse. When roads become clogged by congestion, buses stop, too, whereas a rail transit system can move large numbers of people efficiently on its separate right-of-way.

To create more diverse transportation networks, cities need more choices on how they may spend their federal highway funds. Fortunately, the federal Intermodal Transportation Efficiency Act of 1991 (ISTEA, reauthorized in 1998 as the Transportation Efficiency Act of the 21st Century, or TEA-21) begins to provide cities with flexibility to spend highway moneys on bike paths, train stations, and road improvements that help pedestrians as well as drivers. If we can continue this promising trend, and in particular balance our roads with rail, we can overhaul our transit systems for a more livable 21st century.

"There is magic to great streets. We are attracted to the best of them not because we have to go there but because we want to go there. The best are as joyful as they are utilitarian. They are entertaining and they are open to all. They permit anonymity at the same time as individual recognition. They are symbols of a community and of its history; they represent a public memory. They are places for escape and for romance, places to act and to dream. On a great street we are allowed to dream; to remember things that may never have happened and to look forward to things that, maybe, never will."

ALLAN JACOBS
Great Streets

JOHN O. NORQUIST

John O. Norquist has been Mayor of Milwaukee since 1988. He also is a board member of CNU.

Fifteen

Appropriate building densities and land uses should be within walking distance of transit stops, permitting public transit to become a viable alternative to the automobile.

WILLIAM LIEBERMAN

In many urban areas today, transit is used primarily by people without cars. Public transportation must do its best to serve environments created for the automobile, with characteristics that are antagonistic to the needs of people walking to and from transit stops.

Until the end of the first World War, travel within America's urban areas was primarily on foot or by public transportation. Proximity to public transit was a highly regarded attribute for real estate, as it minimized walking distance. More intense land uses, such as shops, schools, and workplaces, tended to be located around transit stops. Residential densities generally were highest along the streets served by streetcars and buses, tapering to lower densities as the distance from stops increased.

With the advent of the automobile, the relationships between transit and land use weakened. As more people switched to auto travel, fewer were affected by the length of the walk to public transportation. Newer suburbs were laid out primarily with the needs of motorists in mind, and very different patterns of density and location prevailed.

In fact, many of the residential developments laid out in the past 30 years have their lowest densities on the very streets served by buses and light rail. Often this is because the only suitable through streets are large arterials. The levels of noise and pollution generated along these thoroughfares make them poor places for residential

WHEN DENVER'S 16TH STREET was served by trolleys (left), it was the city's main thoroughfare for shopping and entertainment. In the 1960s (center), auto traffic clogged the street and business declined. It was revived as a bus and pedestrian mall in the 1970s (right).

"The road is now like television, violent and tawdry. The landscape it runs through is littered with cartoon buildings and commercial messages. We whiz by them at 55 miles an hour and forget them, because one convenience store looks like the next. They do not celebrate anything beyond their mechanistic ability to sell merchandise. We don't want to remember them. We did not savor the approach and we were not rewarded upon reaching the destination, and it will be the same next time, and every time. There is little sense of having arrived anywhere, because every-place looks like noplace in particular."

JAMES HOWARD KUNSTLER
The Geography of Nowhere

development. Where residential development exists, it often is set back or walled off from the street. Commercial development along these streets also is set back, to allow space for parking. The result is that transit stops are isolated from the developments they were designed to serve and subject to extreme noise and fumes. Densities adjacent to stops there-fore are low, and transit patrons must walk farther to reach their destinations.

Some urban areas have taken a different approach to public transportation. They realize that they strengthen their economic viability and resilience with diverse transportation networks. Transit is treated as a precious resource.

One way to make transit an attractive option is to return to a lesson learned earlier in this century: Minimize the distance that patrons must walk. Shops or offices can be located close to bus and rail stations, thereby increasing the density of surrounding development.

What is a practical walking distance to and from a transit stop? Here are some guidelines: For a bus stop, many residents are willing to walk one-quarter mile. For light rail or rapid transit, patrons will walk somewhat farther—one-third to one-half mile.

There are, however, several caveats. The first is that acceptable walking distances can vary from one community to the next. In cities with extensive

reliance on transit systems and safe, appealing pedestrian routes, walking distances can be greater. A rugged topography or harsh climate can reduce those distances. Second, evidence suggests that patrons will tolerate longer walking distances between transit stops and their homes than they will between transit stops and their workplaces, shops, or other major destinations.

It also should be noted that these distances describe "catchment" areas from which a reasonable proportion of residents can be expected to use transit; the distribution of transit patrons within those areas, however, isn't uniform. It's no surprise that the greatest number of riders live or work quite close to the transit stop, tapering to fewer and fewer as distances increase. It's important, therefore, to site major activity centers such as a community center or shops as close as possible to transit stops, regardless of the size of the catchment area.

Appropriate land uses in these transit-served areas are easier to identify than the densities them-selves. For residential uses adjacent to transit stops, multi-family and rowhouses are preferred over con-ventional single-family homes because the higher densities allow more residents shorter walking dis-tances. Higher-density housing designs also tend to be more resilient to the noise and disruption of busy streets used as major transit routes.

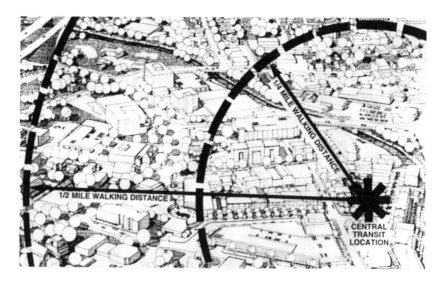

In most communities, at least 18 homes per acre is ideal within a half-mile walk of rail or bus stations, while 12 units per acre is a reasonable minimum density within one-quarter mile of a bus stop. For more suburban, single-family neighborhoods, five to seven units per acre is the lowest viable density for a bus route. These density guidelines can be increased substantially in urban centers and in large cities with extensive transit systems.

Offices should be located directly adjacent to transit stops so employees can use transit conveniently. Minimum floor-area ratios (FAR) of 0.35 to 0.50 are desirable near bus stops, increasing to 1.00 or more near rail stations. (A floor-area ratio is the relationship between the permitted floor area of a building and the area of the lot on which it is located; the higher the FAR, the more intense the use of the parcel.)

For commercial retail, the type of use is more important than the density. Neighborhood retail, such as dry cleaners and cafes, and services like day-care centers, can support transit facilities by providing conveniences close to where riders get on or off. Large retail facilities such as shopping centers can become transit focal points when they are close to transit facilities. The key is for transit stops to be located near the entrances of the buildings, not at the fringes of the parking area. Schools

of any size are ideal near public transportation. For industrial uses, only those that are labor-intensive, rather than space-intensive, should be placed close to transit stops.

Land-use plans and zoning codes that specify these types of uses and densities around existing transit lines—or streets where transit is likely to be built in the future—will go a long way toward transforming urban areas into places where transit contributes to a lively environment. If public transportation can handle a larger portion of travel, urban areas can reduce auto emissions and fuel consumption, and avoid the higher costs associated with building and supporting the infrastructure needed in sprawled land-use patterns. Just as important, the quality of life improves for residents of metropolitan areas when they can choose from among a variety of travel modes and reduce their travel expenses.

PEOPLE WILL WALK A QUARTER-MILE to catch a bus, but when rail transit is available and the route is pleasant, they'll walk up to half a mile. Too many transit stops are engulfed by parking lots and freeways rather than compatible development that supports ridership.

WILLIAM LIEBERMAN

William Lieberman is director of planning and operations for San Diego's Metropolitan Transit Development Board, a legislatively created transit authority that owns and runs systems for light rail and bus. He is the former chair of CNU's Transportation Task Force.

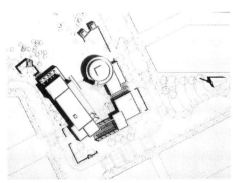

IN TUCSON, ARIZONA, THE NEW CIVANO NEIGHBORHOOD places civic
buildings and services within a short walk of every home. The City of Tucson
permitted development on the condition that Civano consume only two-thirds
the water and energy of a conventional subdivision.

Sixteen

Concentrations of civic, institutional, and commercial activity should be embedded in neighborhoods and districts, not isolated in remote, single-use complexes. Schools should be sized and located to enable children to walk or bicycle to them.

ELIZABETH MOULE

One of the most compelling aspects of the New Urbanism is its recognition that the spatial ordering of uses in our urban environment has such a profound effect on our social, economic, and civic life. What we have learned from the suburban model of automobile-scaled aggregates of single-use zones is that they have had a profoundly negative effect on the quality of our lives — most disproportionately on the lives of women, the economically and physically disadvantaged, the elderly, and children.

The conventional suburban practice of separating land uses by "zones" is the legacy of early industrial workplaces that were once of genuine concern to public welfare. Today, since most industry and commercial activities are benign, few industries need to be separated from other uses. That this approach remains institutionalized in zoning ordinances nationwide overlooks the importance of the natural integration of daily activities. The model of creating a fine-grained mix of uses, with civic, institutional, and commercial located within easy walking distance of each other, provides the greatest accessibility of daily activities to the greatest number of people.

At the scale of the neighborhood, the current model of suburban sprawl is designed to best serve the affluent single adult.

The isolation of most uses in large single-use complexes makes them all but impossible to access by foot and has led to the average person today making 12 car trips daily for work, schools, and shopping.

MOST SUBURBAN DEVELOPMENT (top) isolates women, the economically and physically disadvantaged, the elderly, and children. Fine-grained traditional development allows many people to walk to their daily activities.

"Pushing a stroller along the sidewalk, you naturally meet the eyes of other parents similarly occupied; after running into them again and again at the butcher's, the bakery, the supermarket, you're bound to strike up acquaintance-ships. You can't make those kinds of connections when all your travel time is spent in a car, your shopping done in a vast mall nowhere near your home. When I talk to new mothers who live in the suburbs, the emotion they most often express is a paralyzing feeling of loneliness and isolation. This sentiment is not unknown to urban mothers, but the density of cities mitigates it."

WENDY SMITH

Preservation

The numbers of hours spent in the car are much higher for women, who are most often required not only to work, but also to shuttle children to school and activities while doing most of the household shopping. A reduction of daily car trips is essential to give us all enough time in the day to handle the needs of working, raising a family, seeing friends, giving spiritual sustenance, and making civic contributions to our community.

Ever larger increments of development have a particularly damaging effect on travel patterns. "Megastores" in large single-use shopping areas often cite the need to lower distribution costs as a way of being able to reduce product prices. This is done by locating fewer stores with greater distances between them. The net effect is that these stores have placed the burden of distribution on the watch and gas pedal of every consumer. The real cost of this so-called "efficient" distribution model is the waste of each shopper's time and the ensuing soiling of our environment that all of this travel entails.

These patterns affect all of our lives. Children spend far too much of their time in cars and are unable to be self-reliant users of their environment. The elderly suffer from their inability to remain independent and able to carry out the functions of their daily lives on their own. With very few exceptions, those who do not have the means to own a car find themselves victims of long hours spent in inadequate public transportation systems.

At the scale of the region, the suburban model of isolated zones becomes even more debilitating. With workplaces disproportionately located in city centers and residences mostly located at regional edges, the daily auto commutes for some have reached 100 miles each way, requiring commuters to spend five hours a day behind the wheel.

The oft-bemoaned "loss of community" is only one small price that we all pay for the time we spend isolated in our cars for hours on end. With working parents so far removed from their jobs, children often suffer up to 13 straight hours of day care. Teenagers at home alone are contributing to the rise of gang activity. The effect on families working so far away is mostly fatigue and frustration. However, it has also dissolved marriages, unraveled families, and led to incidents of domestic violence and child abuse, often at rates twice as high as in areas where the distances between home and work are far less. With broken families often come homes being lost. These trends are leading to some of the nation's highest rates of foreclosure and abandoned homes.

At the same time, large concentrations of housing in areas far removed from workplaces and shopping have led to empty neighborhoods during the day that are easy prey for thieves and vandals without the "eyes on the street" that would contribute to safety and security. Moreover, a recent study by the American Farmland Trust has found that emergency response times in large-lot subdivisions far exceed national standards.

Children are the group that suffers most under our current suburban land development patterns. Our cities and towns should be scaled to their use. For children, a strong sense of self-esteem and self-respect develops from their ability to accomplish tasks in a free yet supportive and safe environment. The neighborhood life of a child should be part of a child development continuum based on the individual's self-initiated ability to accomplish his own daily needs.

Children should be able to freely access their environment to meet their needs without depending on others to take them places by automobile. They should gain independence within an environment where they are accountable to others under the rein of both parents and the larger community. Mixed-use streets properly designed with major windows and doorways facing the public right-of-way provide the eyes-on-the-street security that enables a safe environment.

The quality and character of schools is very often cited as the primary reason families choose their place of residence. Sizing schools to the neighborhood reinforces the neighborhood structure and induces greater parental support with the school by making it even more tied to its community. Schools also act as an important community focus. They can form the heart of a neighborhood center with other complementary uses around them, such as day-care centers, parks, grocery stores, and telecommuting centers. As such, they should be

easily accessible to those who use them. Elementary schools should be sized to accommodate the walking population around them; high schools should be sized to accommodate the bicycling population around them.

The late architect Aldo Rossi, who can be credited with renewing our interest in the city as a physically designed object in its own right, produced many schools early in his career. However, many of these schools were located out in the countryside. Rossi believed that the city had an important symbolic function as a pedagogical tool. It is now time to make the real cities not merely symbolic but actual pedagogical tools. And, with a reversal of Rossi's ordering system, schools and other civic buildings need to play their time-honored role of informing and representing society's values—deeply embedded in the hearts of our cities.

"…Public policy should encourage compact, pedestrian-scale development with shopping, services, and employment close to home. If we follow this course, many other benefits are likely to follow. Communities would be less fragmented. Parents would be less coerced to spend their leisure time as chauffeurs for their offspring. Children would have more opportunities to become self-reliant and to gain experiences that prepare them for responsible adulthood. The elderly would find fewer obstacles to staying in their longtime neighborhoods. Neighborhoods might become more stable and vigorous, offering their inhabitants welcome relief from the increasing stresses of modern life."

PHILIP LANGDON
A Better Place to Live

ELIZABETH MOULE

Elizabeth Moule is an architect and principal of Moule & Polyzoides Architects and Urbanists in Pasadena, California. She has taught at many universities as a visiting critic and has written extensively on architecture and urbanism. She is a founding board member of CNU.

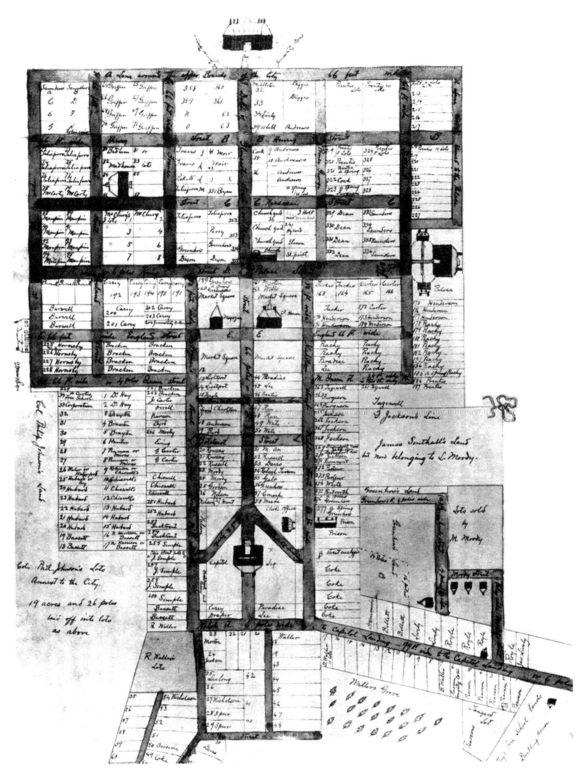

PERHAPS THE FINEST AMERICAN CITY CODE is the ordinance for Colonial Williamsburg, which established the major roads and public building sites and included a six-foot front setback on which buildings were to "front alike," with the requirement for garden walls or fences along the sidewalks.

Seventeen

The economic health and harmonious evolution of neighbor-hoods, districts, and corridors can be improved through graphic urban design codes that serve as predictable guides for change.

BILL LENNERTZ

Throughout history, codes and ordinances have been responsible for maintaining a consistently high quality in the architecture of the street, despite periods of change. An elegant building code has controlled development along the avenues of Paris since the mid-1800s. Perhaps the finest American city code is the ordinance for Colonial Williamsburg, which established the major roads and public building sites and included a six-foot front setback on which buildings were to "front alike," with the requirement for garden walls or fences along the sidewalks.

Codes are pervasive in their control of the built public realm—our streets, parks, and squares, and the buildings that face them. From the finest streets of a historic urban neighborhood to the most barren commercial strips of the suburbs, most build-ing and site design is prescribed by codes. It's therefore not a question of whether to control land development, but rather what to control, and to what end.

As cities grow without proper codes, neighborhoods are subject to incompatible architecture, which causes concern among residents. One underpinning of the New Urbanism is the compatibility of building types—or buildings with the same relative mass, height, and architectural styles, regardless of their uses, which may change over time. Building types are considered compatible when they assure privacy, security, and a consistent quality of street frontage.

IN GAITHERSBURG, MARYLAND, Kentlands (right) is a community created under the guidance of strong codes. Parking and location codes (bottom) for Wilsonville, Oregon.

"In general, most zoning codes are proscriptive. They just try to prevent things from happening, without offering a vision of how things should be. Our codes are prescriptive. We want the streets to feel and act a certain way."

ELIZABETH PLATER-ZYBERK quoted by James Howard Kunstler in *The Geography of Nowhere*

New Urbanism supports the idea of a visual and functional coherence that protects the quality of the street life. Codes must achieve a delicate balance of assuring compatibility (listing permissible building types and codifying how buildings must relate to each other and the street) without inhibiting creativity (buildings should read as distinct and have individual character). In a town built without the benefit of centuries of architectural traditions or a diversity of founders, codes should encourage variety while ensuring the harmony that gives a community character.

One of the greatest challenges for cities is transforming single-use and single-density districts into mixed-use neighborhoods. Instead of offering reactionary defenses against separate, incompatible buildings, codes should guide the building of diverse and mixed-use places. The difficulty arises in locating different building types, which for

decades have been separate, closer to one another. During this period of divorce, building types that once were compatible have become estranged. Courtyard apartment buildings that comfortably occupied the corners of single-family streets have become segregated as garden apartment complexes. The neighborhood corner store has become the drive-in convenience mart on the commercial strip. As they currently exist, these building types are compatible only with themselves; they no longer belong within the neighborhood.

CODES

Building New Urbanist communities may require creating new codes or changing existing zoning codes, urban design codes, and building and architectural codes. Codes can direct the transformation toward mixed neighborhoods by regulating the elements that make disparate building types visually and functionally compatible. Urban design codes contained within town or city ordinances regulate elements such as private building footprints and heights related to the formation of public spaces. Architectural codes administered by developers address architectural details, such as style, materials, and construction techniques. Together, these codes can determine the elements of private buildings that affect the architecture of the street, such as front setback, garage placement, mass of the facade, and the placement of entrances, porches, and windows.

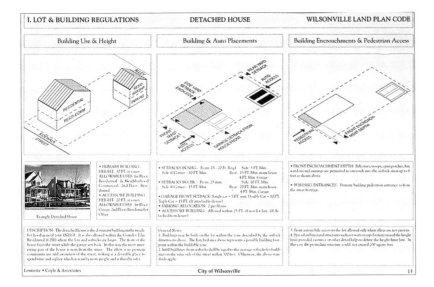

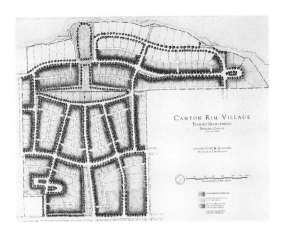

THE REGULATING

PLAN for the Canyon

Rim Neighborhood

in Redmond, Oregon.

Architectural codes often are private covenants initiated by land developers for particular projects (one exception is historic districts, which may have their own architectural codes determined by a city, town, or district). Ideally, architectural codes are crafted by consensus among the developer, town planners, and the local jurisdiction, and are put in place as part of the deed restrictions. These codes, combined with covenants and restrictions (known collectively as CC&Rs), are administered by such entities as master developers and homeowner associations. CC&Rs are private agreements and may be quite prescriptive in detail.

The New Urbanism recommends that the following items be included in site-specific codes:

- the regulating plan, showing the platting of the various zones (the countryside, corridors, neighborhoods, and districts), the public rights-of-way, (thoroughfares, civic building lots, open spaces), and private lots. In an already developed area, the layout of lots and street rights-of-way, for example, can be incorporated into a city code.

- use standards that locate the allowed uses of buildings in various zones.

- urban regulations that control those aspects of private buildings that affect public space, such as building height and placement, location of primary entrances, location of parking, and encouragements for stoops and porches.

- architectural regulations that assure visual compatibility among disparate building types by controlling building materials and configurations.

- thoroughfare standards that control the dimensions of vehicular and pedestrian ways that are specialized in both capacity and character. For existing streets, standards should show options for retrofits.

- landscape standards, with planting prescriptions for public and private land, to maintain a visually coherent urban fabric.

ORDINANCES

Ordinances are local laws for land development adopted by a public governing agency. Since ordinances are usually required to be "clear and prescriptive," they normally are less controlling of architectural and design elements than private codes. Ordinances include a city's land-use or zoning code, which regulates the physical aspects of land development according to use, building placement and bulk, parking provisions, and landscape. The intention of ordinances is to create compatible neighborhoods and to protect public safety, health, and welfare.

"The most important features of city planning are not the public buildings, not the railroad approaches, not even the parks and playgrounds. They are the location of streets, the establishment of block lines, the subdivisions of property into lots, the regulations of building, and the housing of people.... The fixing and extension of these features is too often left practically without effective regulation to the decision of private individuals. That these individuals are often lacking in knowledge, in taste, in high or even fair civic motives; that they are often controlled by ignorance, caprice, and selfishness, the present character of American city suburbs bears abundant testimony."

JOHN NOLEN

city planner, on his 1911 plan for Madison, Wisconsin

IMPLEMENTATION STRATEGIES

Through a process of citizen participation, cities and towns should examine the ability of their ordinances to create mixed-use neighborhoods, districts, and corridors. If those ordinances don't allow for mixed-use places, planners and citizens should develop a strategy for revising them in one of the following ways:

- Start over. Completely rewrite the city's comprehensive plan and zoning ordinances with the help of neighborhood associations, local developers, business leaders, and city staff. Create a new vision for the city and a strategy for how to achieve and maintain that vision.

- Adopt a set of parallel ordinances. Keep the current ordinances but also offer an alternate track that will produce a mixed-use neighborhood. In some communities, for example, an overlay allows developers the choice of creating a New Urbanist development (typical design overlays address issues such as reducing the domination of the garage door on the street and the location of building entrances on a public way). Encourage the alternative track by providing faster plan approval or other incentives. This approach often is more easily accepted politically, and therefore can be adopted relatively quickly.

- Rewrite selected portions of the ordinances. Identify the major code obstacles and rewrite only those problem sections. This approach may be necessary to change quickly regulations that are responsible for a rapid erosion of the quality of a community (when a shopping-mall strip is proposed, for example). These rewritten ordinances should be included in a town or city's comprehensive plan, which establishes the guiding planning principles and policies that describe the city's composition of neighborhoods, districts and corridors, and countryside.

In New Urbanist communities, ordinances can shape a public space, and the architectural codes make the buildings around it compatible and add another layer of richness and character. Another way of thinking about this is that ordinances will make a town, and architectural codes will make a beautiful town. Given the power of codes in determining the harmonious evolution and economic stability of places, creating urban-design codes that ensure diverse, mixed-use neighborhoods and towns will help guide these communities through change.

BILL LENNERTZ

Bill Lennertz is a founder and principal of Lennertz Coyle & Associates, architects and town planners in Portland, Oregon. He was co-editor for *Andres Duany and Elizabeth Plater-Zyberk: Towns and Town-Making Principles* (Harvard University Graduate School of Design, 1991). Lennertz is a founding member of CNU.

Eighteen

A range of parks, from tot lots and village greens to ballfields and community gardens, should be distributed within neighborhoods. Conservation areas and open lands should be used to define and connect different neighborhoods and districts.

THOMAS J. COMITTA

In the Manayunk section of Philadelphia, where I grew up, residents can stroll through the one-half-acre Pretzel Park (right), play ball at Hillside Park, walk along a canal towpath, or bicycle to Fairmount Park. This network of green spaces is complemented by common areas along Main Street, including small, tree-lined parks that provide opportunities for relaxation and conversation, and the Venice Island playground, which offers recreational opportunities such as basketball, ice skating, swimming, and rollerblading. Life in the Manayunk neighborhood is pleasant because of a system of parks and open spaces that gives this place a special character and helps define and connect it with other neighborhoods.

PROVIDING GRACE AND BALANCE

Consider some of our most memorable parks—New York's Central Park, the Boston Commons, or Lincoln Park in Washington, D.C. They are remarkable largely because they provide attractive spaces around which neighborhoods flourish and derive special meaning. In vibrant traditional cities, we find park systems that provide opportunities for leisure, exercise, culture, scenery, and public space. In traditional towns and neighborhoods, we find diversified places for passive and active recreation—parks and open spaces that provide a grace and balance to the community.

Neighborhoods appear as balanced living environments when parks are the linchpin of a community. Neighborhoods also appear balanced spatially when buildings are

The Milwaukee RiverWalk: Revitalizing the Central City

ONCE THE MILWAUKEE RIVER WAS A POLLUTED DITCH running through the heart of the city. After the water quality was improved through advanced sewage treatment, the city launched a $10 million effort to create a series of riverfront parks, landings, plazas, and promenades. The Milwaukee RiverWalk has proven highly successful. Buildings that turned their back on the river have been renovated with new cafes

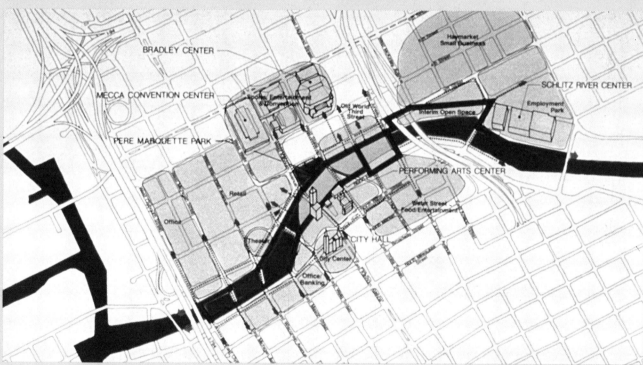

and restaurants facing the water. The promenades and water-taxi stands have knit together civic, residential, entertainment, convention, and business elements of downtown. In 1996, the RiverWalk's Pere Marquette Park even hosted a celebration including President Bill Clinton and German Chancellor Helmut Kohl. Efforts are under way to extend the RiverWalk into other downtown districts.

"Since most production in
the city takes place under a
roof, indoors, it is obvious
that urban recreation must
emphasize the out-of-doors,
plant life, air, and light.
In our poorly mechanized,
over-centralized, and
congested cities the crying
need is for organized space:
flexible, adaptable outdoor
space in which to stretch,
breath, expand, grow."
GARRETT ECKBO,
DANIEL U. KILEY, AND
JAMES C. ROSE
*Landscape Design in the
Urban Environment*

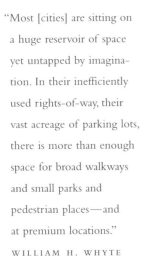

"Most [cities] are sitting on
a huge reservoir of space
yet untapped by imagina-
tion. In their inefficiently
used rights-of-way, their
vast acreage of parking lots,
there is more than enough
space for broad walkways
and small parks and
pedestrian places—and
at premium locations."
WILLIAM H. WHYTE

complemented by plazas, squares, and other open
spaces. The contrast between built and unbuilt
is attractive on several levels: between the firm
textures of buildings and streets and the soft colors
and textures of the natural world; between a
more formal architectural character and nature's
informality; and between the massing of structures
and the openness of common space. With parks
and other open spaces to provide visually
stimulating contrasts, both the architectural and
natural environments in a neighborhood read
as more distinguished.

GIVING FORM TO THE NEIGHBORHOOD

Within a traditional neighborhood, the form of
open spaces should relate directly to the network of
streets and lanes. As larger green spaces, the market
plaza, the civic plaza, the green, the park, and the
edge should all relate to the design of the whole
neighborhood. As smaller green spaces, the playground, the close, and the square should all relate
to the design of the block. The ideal traditional
neighborhood typically involves contact with a
park, plaza, square, or village green within a five-
to-ten-minute walk of its center (these elements
often are located within the center). Within a
quarter-mile radius from the center of a traditional
neighborhood, there typically are other green or
civic places such as a tot lot, playgrounds, playfields,
or community gardens.

Raymond Unwin's 1909 book, *Town Planning
in Practice*, describes the role of "places" with civic
and green space as the form-giving element of the
traditional town. Unwin recommended planning

a neighborhood that wasn't exclusively buildings,
but also provided common open spaces. What
motivated Unwin's ideas from the late 1800s were
overcrowding and squalid conditions in the city of
London. His call for city neighborhoods to incorporate fresh air, light, and visual relief was echoed
by other planners and social reformers, in large
part for public health reasons, but also for aesthetic
and civic reasons. His notion of giving discipline to
the space used for civic and recreation purposes—
carefully planning the arrangement of parks and
other green spaces to create an attractive contrast
and balance—contributes to the town planning
tradition that now allows us the pleasure of
discovering a vest-pocket park or small plaza.

Through the Garden City concept advanced
by Ebenezer Howard in his 1898 book, *Garden
Cities of To-morrow,* the core of a settlement is considered organized and memorable when the space
in the center is devoted to and maintained as a
park-like setting. When the edge of a settlement
is open and green, it promotes a distinct contrast
with the built environment. This is shown in the
diagram of Howard's "Ward and Centre Garden-
City"(on page 44).

SUPPORTING AND CELEBRATING
NEIGHBORHOOD LIFE

Parks and open areas are the places that support
neighborhood life and its celebrations. The Fourth
of July picnic, Halloween "dark in the park," and
the summer concert series all happen in the park.
What gives each park special character are features

such as the veterans memorial, the water fountain, the civic leader monument, the memorial bench, the playfield, and the tree-lined walkway. These elements and furnishings give parks a distinct meaning and address within individual neighborhoods.

Although the suburban-sprawl pattern of development has not retained the park as one of the main organizing principles for the neighborhood, vestiges of "green" can be found at schools and neighborhood and community parks. These parks often serve as the only form in the suburbs of what Ray Oldenburg calls "the great good place," in his 1989 book of the same name. Oldenburg's premise is that vital neighborhoods and towns offer three realms: home, the workplace, and the great good place, an informal gathering spot—such as a park, community center, coffee shop, or bar— where people create and celebrate community. While sprawl-type development doesn't generally include places for casual social mixing, suburban parks over the next century will provide valuable anchors and enclaves that could help redefine and reshape those neighborhoods.

One outcome of the rapid suburbanization and depletion of natural resources over the past 50 years is that the public has become aware of the vital role that green spaces have in our quality of life. Parks enhance neighborhood life by providing needed green space, trees, light, and air. Community gardens provide a direct connection to the earth and to producing food and flowers needed for our physical and spiritual sustenance. Open spaces, large

and small, offer opportunities to observe wildlife and participate in natural cycles.

Thanks to the environmental sensitivities expressed in the 1970s and 1980s, we have become more conscious of designating greenways, riparian buffers, wildlife corridors, and other open lands. Besides enhancing the environmental health of a neighborhood and providing a universal link with nature, the greenbelt, the greensward, and the countryside also clearly define human settlements and distinguish them from one another. Larger conservation areas and open lands shape and connect different neighborhoods and communities.

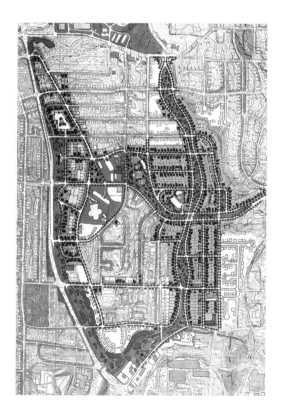

"I never learned to doubt that the city was part of nature.... Cities must resist the habit of fragmenting nature. Only by viewing the entire natural environment as one interacting system can the value of nature be fully appreciated."
ANNE WHISTON SPIRN
The Granite Garden

A NEW LINEAR PARK was created for Kimberly Park HOPE VI redevelopment in Winston-Salem, North Carolina. The park provides a shared focus of amenities for the neighborhood and connects adjacent neighborhoods.

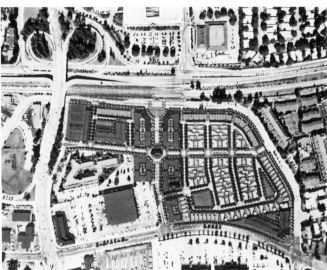

TOO OFTEN, NEW PARKS are oversized and placed beyond walking distance of most residents. In Mountain View, California, The Crossings, a new neighborhood made on the site of a dead mall (upper left), places small parks throughout the 18-acre site (plan view, upper right). Parks are included in a system of pathways leading to a light-rail station.

PLANNING FOR PARKS AND OPEN SPACES
Development policies and codes increasingly are being fine-tuned to present the right formula for the built and the unbuilt environments. Within many traditional neighborhoods, a range of between 8 percent and 15 percent of the landscape is typically reserved for "green spaces" for recreational and leisure pursuits. Within a town or community, a range from 25 percent to 40 percent of the landscape is typically reserved for environmental conservation and recreation.

Parks and open spaces should be distributed within neighborhoods, and should be created and maintained to help define and connect neighborhoods. Parks and open spaces can be designed and organized according to their spatial attributes and their functions.

As part of a network of green and open spaces, the function of the park system should include: the "green" formed by surrounding streets, with buildings oriented around it; the tot lot or mini-park; the playground with play equipment and courts; the playfield and athletic field; the community park shared by a group of neighborhoods with a pavilion, amphitheater, or gazebo; the community gardens; the greenway or open space corridor on the edge of neighborhoods; and the countryside between towns consisting in large part of agricultural land and other open space.

As the principles of the New Urbanism become more widely practiced, good neighborhoods and towns will be defined by an integrated network of parks and open spaces. When strung together with places for living, working, shopping, and civic activities, parks can provide, borrowing the idea popularized by the great landscape architect Frederick Law Olmsted, an "emerald necklace" for the neighborhood.

"Sandboxes and playgrounds don't work just for kids. Some of my best friends are those I met when I watched over my sons' play in sandboxes of Riverside Drive in New York City. The streets adjacent to Riverside Drive, which had no strips of park to accommodate such play areas, had much less social life."

AMITAI ETZIONI
The Spirit of Community

THOMAS J. COMITTA

Thomas J. Comitta, AICP, RLA, ASLA, is president of Thomas Comitta Associates, Inc., a town planning and landscape architecture firm in West Chester, Pennsylvania. He is also co-chair of CNU's Standards & Precedents Task Force and has prepared livable community design standards for many municipalities.

BLOCK, STREET, AND BUILDING

The Charter's smallest scale is the Block, the Street, and the Building. At this scale, we need to accommodate automobiles as well as pedestrians. New Urbanism does not naively call for the elimination of the car. Rather, it challenges us to create environments that support walking, biking, transit, and the car. This section outlines urban design strategies that reinforce human scale while incorporating contemporary realities. Jobs no longer need to be isolated in office parks, but their integration into mixed-use neighborhoods calls for sensitive urban design. Different types of housing no longer need buffers to separate and isolate them, but they do need architecture that signifies continuity within the neighborhood. Retail and civic uses do not need special zones, but they do need block, street, and building patterns that connect them to their community.

Daniel Solomon launches this exploration by delimiting the fault line between Modernism and the traditional urbanism that continues to flourish. Stefanos Polyzoides explains why style may be irrelevant, although responding to historical and other contextual settings is crucial. Ray Gindroz and Tony Hiss illuminate the connection between physical design and public safety—and why it involves much more than bright lighting and strong policing. Arguing that pedestrian-only environments can be economic and social failures, Douglas Farr explains how autos can be threaded into safe and lively streets and public spaces. Victor Dover identifies the patterns that make streets and public plazas successful. In additional commentary, Gianni Longo explains how we can advance efforts to restore public spaces. Douglas Kelbaugh proposes new means to root new buildings to their natural, cultural, and historical settings. Regarding civic buildings, Andres Duany says that planning and foresight are more important than architecture—but that exuberant design can provide vital symbolism. Mark Schimmenti discusses the continuing importance of the natural elements in a climate-controlled world, while Ken Greenberg says we must not lose sight of the need to identify, protect, and revitalize historic areas.

Nineteen

A primary task of all urban architecture and landscape design is the physical definition of streets and public spaces as places of shared use.

DANIEL SOLOMON

This principle addresses the clearest difference between typical building patterns of the recent past and virtually the whole of urban history from Neolithic villages until World War II. The late 20th-century spatial flux of parking lots, autonomous buildings, and formless in-betweens is familiar to everyone on the planet, but scarcely existed two brief generations ago.

Anyone who thinks that urban squares are obsolete, or that traditional, figural spaces clearly shaped and defined by buildings are somehow irrelevant to the economic and social forces now at work in the American city, should take a look at San Francisco's South Park. It is a little urban square, measuring 160 by 600 feet, with rounded ends like a miniature Piazza Navona. Except on cold, windy days, the space is crowded with the young, hip citizens of the city's Multimedia Gulch—a decidedly up-to-the-minute industry that is helping to fuel San Francisco's remarkable prosperity. They have been drawn to South Park and they have adopted it as their own because it is a beautiful space—just the right size, consistently defined by buildings that are interesting in their own right, but not too interesting, and with a mix of uses around it that includes some good restaurants, a welding shop, galleries, and dwellings that range from subsidized single-room occupancy hotels (SROs) to luxury condos.

The park itself is no masterpiece, but it has some London Plane trees of good size, benches to sit on, and places for kids. It is surrounded by a narrow one-way street with parking on both sides. No one ever drives faster than 10 miles an hour. You can cross

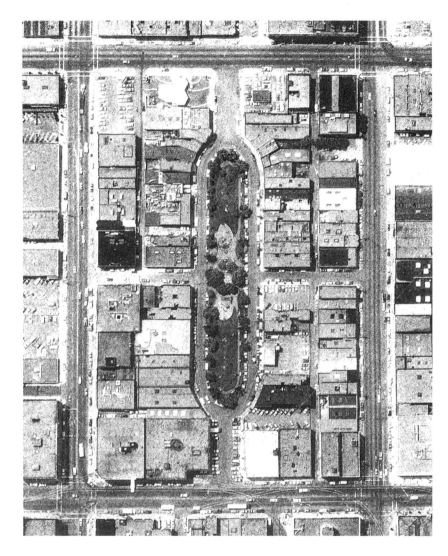

CARVED FROM FOUR CITY BLOCKS, San Francisco's South Park demonstrates
how buildings and streets define public space. In the heart of booming Multimedia
Gulch, traffic never exceeds 10 miles an hour, and people always have a place to play,
to sit in the shade of a London Plane tree, or to launch a cross-town stroll.

the narrow street anywhere. South Park is carved from the middle of four standard city blocks, the simple act of a 19th-century entrepreneur who saw it as a way to create a place out of no place and thereby make some money for himself. Sometimes New Urbanism is just a matter of not forgetting old knowledge.

The liberation of architecture and landscape from their traditional civic duties as the walls, portals, and passages of the public realm is a recent phenomenon that tends to displace what has stood as shared wisdom for millennia. It has been brought about by pressures common throughout the world. The automobile has the largest role in this story, but there are also other factors at work. The roots of modern architecture in object-making, buildings as "machines for living" whose sole allegiances are to their own programs and technics, have made their own huge contributions to the crisis of place so visible at the frayed edges of cities everywhere. New Urbanists regard this condition of formlessness as neither beneficial nor irreversible.

The continued vitality, popularity, and economic health of traditional urban streets and squares defined by their buildings is significant in this regard. Late 20th-century planners, architects, developers, and bureaucrats may have lost track of how collectively to construct a proper public realm, but late 20th-century people have clearly not forgotten how to use it, to depend upon it and to take great pleasure in its qualities. There are many beautiful and physically intact traditional urban places that accommodate automobiles and

the same economic life as the most formless, edge-city sprawl. New Urbanism is predicated upon the principle that there is no inherent and necessary connection between the rise of an electronic information culture and the disintegration of urban form.

The precursors of New Urbanism began in the 1970s to evolve methods of analysis and design, suitable to our contemporary circumstance, that restore the traditional reciprocity between the form of buildings and the form of public space. The methods of depicting urban space developed by Belgian architect Rob Krier, the 1978 publication of the classic book *Collage City* by Colin Rowe and Fred Koetter, the publication of *Court and Garden* by Michael Dennis in 1986, and the evolution of the figure-ground method of drawing urban form at Cornell and many other schools are milestones in this evolution. It is unlikely that a generation of planners, architects, and landscape architects accustomed to the convention of figure-ground representation of urban contexts will ever grant the same autonomy to buildings that was typical in the heyday of the Modern movement. This way of drawing makes the urban damage (right) inflicted by autonomous and self-referential buildings too obvious to ignore.

Beginning with theoretical groundwork laid out so vividly in the texts quoted on these pages, many architects and planners have found practical means to ensure that buildings reassert their traditional role as the definers of public space. One simple but crucial shift in planning practice has been the supplanting of the term *setback* with

"[B]y 1930, the disintegration of the street and of all highly organized public space seemed to have become inevitable; and for two major reasons: the new and rationalized form of housing and the new dictates of vehicular activity. For, if the configuration of housing now evolved from the inside out, from the logical needs of the individual residential unit, then it could no longer be subservient to external pressures; and, if external public space had become so functionally chaotic as to be without effective significance, then—in any case—there were no valid pressures which it could any longer exert."

COLIN ROWE AND
FRED KOETTER
Collage City

"For centuries, space was the principle medium of urbanism—the matrix that united public and private interests in the city, guaranteeing a balance between the two. But in the eighteenth century, a process of change—social, intellectual, and formal—began to alter that balance in favor of the private realm. Freestanding object buildings began to replace enclosed public space as the focus of architectural thought, this formal transformation—from public space to private icon—was finally completed in the early twentieth century. The demise of public realm was then assured.... [A]ny form of rebirth must be accompanied by the reconstitution of the formal setting public life requires."

MICHAEL DENNIS
Court and Garden

the more architectonic term *build-to line*. The setbacks of conventional zoning ordinances prescribe minimum distances from buildings to property lines. They imply buildings that float in a continuous matrix of undifferentiated space. Build-to lines, on the other hand, are specific prescriptions for the shapes of spaces defined by buildings. Requirements for build-to lines can be structured in ways that still permit flexibility for architects to address the programmatic requirements of their buildings, and to give identity and expressive qualities to their individual works. A requirement for a build-to line might say that 60 percent of a street frontage must be built to the property line and another 20 percent of the building must be within 10 feet of the property line. Setbacks imply that buildings are perceived and experienced in-the-round, as freestanding sculptural objects. Build-to lines reestablish the principal of frontality and make buildings parts of larger ensembles defining the public realm.

In addition to the shape and placement of buildings, the characteristics of their surfaces are crucial to the quality of the public spaces they define. The needs for many modern urban buildings to accommodate large parking garages and to be secure from intruders make the task of animating and giving vitality to the public realm more complex than ever before. Both the planning framework for urban buildings and the works of individual architects should ensure that the frontages of public spaces are lined with entrances, retail frontages, and the windows of rooms so that the traditional interdependency between the private life of buildings and the collective life of towns is once more the animating principle of civic design.

DANIEL SOLOMON

A founding member of CNU and member of CNU's Board of Directors, architect Daniel Solomon is a principal in Solomon Architecture and Urban Design in San Francisco. He is also the author of *ReBuilding* (Princeton Architectural Press, 1992) and a professor of architecture at the University of California at Berkeley.

Twenty

Individual architectural projects should be seamlessly linked to their surroundings. This issue transcends style.

STEFANOS POLYZOIDES

The architecture of our time is dominated by obsessively self-referential, isolated projects. Such projects aggrandize the individual interests of their clients. They highlight the formal language and signature of their authors. They endeavor to express in stylistic terms the mood of the cultural instant when they were designed and built.

The typical project today, however big or small, is a commodity that demands a unique, differentiated, and, therefore, superficial image. We are left with a cultural and physical landscape of unprecedented confusion, monotony, and fragility. The battle of the styles fueled by the interests and ambitions of countless clients and their architects is in no small measure responsible.

A temporal architecture, or an architecture of a specific time, that communicates through a stream of hastily designed, undecipherable private projects is by definition ephemeral. When introduced into a long-lived urban or natural setting, this Architecture of Time induces chaos by slowly undermining and eventually destroying by design a cultural commitment to coherence in the city and nature.

In contrast to an Architecture of Time, a New Urbanist architecture is an Architecture of Place. It does not rely upon the idle repetition of historical styles. Instead, New Urbanist architecture strives to evolve by exercising critical design choices across time. Its language and permanence endeavor to express a diverse set of deep values held by those who live in and around it. It is only a fragment of a larger order. Whatever its

"We want no new style of architecture. Who wants a new style of painting or of sculpture? But we want some style."
JOHN RUSKIN

"All styles are good except the boring kind."
VOLTAIRE
The Prodigal Child

ARCHITECTURAL
TYPES and building
designs have evolved for
hundreds of years in dif-
ferent parts of the United
States in response to a
vibrant local culture.

An adobe house in
Taos Pueblo, New
Mexico (below), and a
wooden sideyard house
in Charleston, South
Carolina.

"There was a time in our
past when one could walk
down any street and be
surrounded by harmonious
buildings. Such a street
wasn't perfect, it wasn't
necessarily even pretty, but
it was alive. The old buildings smiled, while our new
buildings are faceless. The
old buildings sang, while
the buildings of our age
have no music in them.

The designers of the
past succeeded easily where
most today fail because
they saw something dif-
ferent when they looked
at a building. They saw a
pattern in light and shade.
When they let pattern
guide them, they opened
their ability to make
forms of rich complexity.
The forms they made
began to dance."
JONATHAN HALE
The Old Way of Seeing

size, a New Urbanist architecture is a mere incre-
ment in the process of completing buildings, streets,
blocks, neighborhoods, districts, corridors, and
natural regions.

A genuine architectural culture can only exist
within the accumulated experience afforded by
historical continuity. For architecture and urbanism
to prosper as disciplines, they need the wisdom and
guidance of enduring values, traditions, methods,
and ideas.

The continuity of place-making is the
critical dimension of a New Urbanist architecture.
Continuity emerges through the thoughtful consid-
eration of various scales of design, and then through
design itself as an integrative and transforming act.
The pursuit of an incremental, seamless engage-
ment with the physical environment supplants
style as the preeminent subject of design. Style is
replaced by a search for form suited to the
harmonious evolution of the city and nature.

OPERATING WITHIN A REGIONAL
FRAMEWORK

This nation's many regional traditions grew from
centuries of design in particular settings, social
cultures, and climates. A New Urbanist architecture
does not result from a single or universal style.
It is a set of principles expressed in the language
of each distinct region. One of its most urgent
priorities is to discover and revitalize through new
design these diverse, if dormant, regional languages
of vernacular design.

DISTINGUISHING BETWEEN DWELLINGS
AND MONUMENTS

The 20th century has seen an impressive level of
confusion in the character of buildings. Houses
are made into monuments, civic buildings become
routine, and commercial buildings are loud
and bombastic.

The design of monuments should differ from
the design of other buildings. Monuments are
foreground, one-off buildings, bound by typological
conventions, yet free to express the unique conditions of each program, site, and institution. They
provide the inflections, the points of reference in
the city and the countryside. By contrast, dwellings
and commercial buildings are bound by the fact
that they are repeated so extensively as to become
the collective form and fabric of the city. Their
design often invites the designer's light intervention
on a known type. They are the background against
which monumental buildings are balanced.

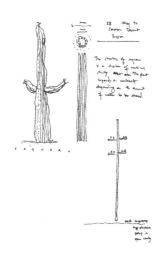

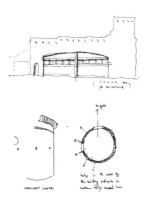

AT THE UNIVERSITY OF ARIZONA in Tucson, the Colonia de la Paz Residence Halls are in a 300-foot-by-300-foot building organized around 11 courtyards as an extension of Hispanic building and town planning traditions. Specific sources were documented in the architect's sketchbooks during the design. A variety of techniques was then incorporated that adapted the building to desert living conditions, including a cooling tower in its principal courtyard.

DECIPHERING A CONTEXT

Authentic design choices emerge by relating to the urban and natural order of existing places. To generate a true Architecture of Place, it is necessary to draw the boundaries of the context of each project, identify the elements of past designs, reveal their physical characteristics, and assess their value and relevance.

DESIGNING BY REFERENCE
TO PRECEDENTS

The architecture of the New Urbanism is more referential than abstract. It depends on historical precedent as guide and inspiration. In each setting for new projects, designers must discover and respect the patterns of buildings, open space, landscape, infrastructure, and transportation networks. These typological precedents are the historical patterns society has employed to resolve formal challenges in recurring programs and sites. They are the living proof of an architectural culture. A typological order, different for each region, is a principal subject that must be mastered before a new project becomes an instrument of positive change.

"Since my early youth I have been acutely aware of the chaotic ugliness of our modern man-made environment when compared to the unity and beauty of old, pre-industrial towns."
WALTER GROPIUS

INTEGRATING FORMAL ELEMENTS

The language of the New Urbanism is not limited to buildings. Every project also contains within its boundaries fragments that define the overall network of roads and parking, infrastructure, open space, and landscape. Each project built then becomes an agent for the harmonious completion of the form of the city and nature.

Buildings added to existing buildings generate a fabric. Open spaces added to existing open spaces define an active public realm. Landscape added to existing landscape introduces the vibrant presence of nature into the city. The character of places depends on the judicious combination of all these elements through design.

RESPONDING TO NATURE

The architecture of the New Urbanism accommodates itself with the forces of nature. A seamless connection to the existing built world is unlikely to be made unless spaces for human habitation, indoors or outdoors, become specific to their place and climate. Designing in response to nature can entail a number of initiatives: minimizing energy use and pollution, maximizing water conservation and management, constructing more permanent buildings with recyclable materials, and promoting renovation, rehabilitation, and reuse.

IN THE EVOLVING DESIGN for the town of Windsor, Florida, an architecture of place is harmoniously accomplished. Many architects designed a neighborhood under a code that prescribed key architectural and urban common elements while allowing freedom of expression.

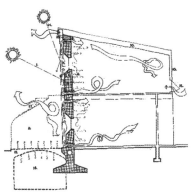

KELBAUGH RESIDENCE in Princeton, New Jersey, is a historic moment in American sustainable architecture: It was the first Trombe wall house in America and one of the first to use passive solar energy.

USING TECHNOLOGY IN THE SERVICE OF ARCHITECTURE

Projects are by definition place-specific when they utilize a process of construction that fits the challenges of diverse local settings. We should reject uniformly, around the world, the pursuit of a capital-intensive, advanced, and expensive materials-based architecture. On the other hand, an Architecture of Place will always use technology in a flexible way to build differently in different settings and times. The availability of relatively cheap labor in some places can produce architecture that emphasizes hand-crafting. In capital-rich settings, an architecture assembled out of machine-fabricated parts can flourish. And in places in between, technology can serve architecture based on many, diverse, and appropriate processes of construction.

CONCLUSION

Style is not an *a priori* dimension of design. Style should emerge from two choices made within a cultural and environmental framework for each region. First, there is the question of adopting, transforming, or denying an existing order of building, open space, landscape, infrastructure, and transportation networks. Second, a decision must be made on the use of an appropriate language of design and building. The available options are traditional, abstract, or hybrid. The first is a matter of public responsibility, the second is a matter of subjective judgment. The consequence of practicing these two choices can be an Architecture of Place based on an aesthetic of formal coherence.

Such an architecture of choosing (*eklegein* in Greek) is in the best sense of the word eclectic. It demands architectural expression in response to different settings. It is based on an evolving common understanding of the structure of places, subject to reinterpretation by each architect. It is incremental rather than revolutionary, respectful rather than avant-garde. By directing designers and builders to the value of what exists, and by encouraging them to operate sensitively and thoughtfully, a New Urbanist architecture itself can ultimately become generative and timeless: as precedent, as invitation to interpretation, and as a point of departure for subsequent design that is both an end and a beginning.

STEFANOS POLYZOIDES

Stefanos Polyzoides is a partner in Moule & Polyzoides Architects and Urbanists in Pasadena, California, and an associate professor of architecture at the University of Southern California. He is a founding board member of CNU.

Twenty one

The revitalization of urban places depends on safety and security. The design of streets and buildings should reinforce safe environments, but not at the expense of accessibility and openness.

RAY GINDROZ

Urban safety is perhaps the most fundamental problem all cities face. No one wants to live, work, start a business, or shop in a city unless it's safe.

Both the perception and reality of a safe and secure environment are essential to attract people to our inner-city neighborhoods. Crime statistics may plummet, but if people feel lost or trapped within a public space, unable to see or find a quick way out, they will avoid it. Public spaces devoid of other people or lined with blank walls or boarded-up windows seem dangerous (and are) because they are not managed or cared for, and are therefore out of control. Gated communities isolate those inside and often make the space around them more dangerous.

Safe places, on the other hand, are orderly, well lit, and clean. Public spaces where we either see or feel others around us make us feel secure. Safe public spaces have well-maintained buildings with windows, and open vistas that show a way out and help us find our way through the city. These spaces seem safe (and are) because they are orderly, cared for, and therefore under control.

Design, once considered only a minor factor in security concerns, is now known to be an essential component of urban safety. New Urbanists recognize that public spaces need to be loved to be safe, and that good design helps support secure urban environments. Design alone, however, is powerless: Community safety and security requires a partnership among designers, community leaders, residents, and community-based police.

THE HUMAN PRESENCE, provided by elements such as front porches, is crucial

for safe streets. This is true within a privately built community like Celebration, Florida

(top), or in mixed public and private housing like the Randolph Neighborhood

(above), or Diggs Town (right), two projects in Virginia.

The issue is not so much how to create spaces that can be defended, but rather how to create spaces that bring people together and keep them safe. In urban areas, the public spaces where street lighting, streetscapes, and paving meet private property must be maintained collaboratively by public and private property owners. This collaboration is accomplished by consensus, which can be fostered by designing spaces that people can identify with, develop a strong sense of ownership for, and be proud of.

SEVEN QUALITIES OF SAFE SPACES

The qualities that support this collaboration for safety include:

1. HUMAN PRESENCE

People in a public space must feel the presence of other people in the space and in the buildings surrounding the space. The sense that we are not alone and are being observed helps us behave properly and feel safe. Windows are symbols of that presence, whether people are behind them or not. Mixed-use buildings help promote 24-hour presence.

2. CONGENIALITY

The dimensions and scale of the space should encourage comfortable interactions among people.

3. HUMANE PROTECTION

Mechanical devices such as cameras and gates should be invisible. Where possible, police presence should be personal, on foot or bicycle, so police officers can interact with others.

4. VISIBILITY, LIGHT, AND OPENNESS

Open views that enable us to see other people and to be seen—by people driving by, as well as by others in the space—provide natural supervision. Lighting should ensure nighttime visibility.

5. ORDER

Coherent landscapes, streetscapes, and signs in both the public rights-of-way and bordering properties make a clear statement that a space is well-managed and safe.

6. CONNECTIONS

Spaces must be perceived as part of an interconnected network of streets and public open space, so we feel we have access to others who make the space safe.

7. LEGIBILITY

The clarity with which each space connects to the rest of the city helps us understand the form of the city, keeps us from feeling lost, and assures us that we are in control of our relationship with the city spaces and the people in them.

APPLYING THE PRINCIPLES TO PUBLIC SPACES

Applying these principles and qualities varies with each type of public space, such as the following:

NEIGHBORHOOD STREETS

A neighborhood street lined with carefully tended front yards, flower-filled porches, and house facades with large windows feels safe and comfortable. A stranger knows that he will be seen and made to feel either welcome or not. The message is clear

"Streets and their sidewalks, the main public places of a city, are its most vital organs. Think of a city and what comes to mind? Its streets. If a city's streets look interesting, the city looks interesting; if they look dull, the city looks dull. More than that... if a city's streets are safe from barbarism and fear, the city is thereby tolerably safe from barbarism and fear. When people say that a city, or part of it, is dangerous or is a jungle what they mean primarily is that they do not feel safe on the sidewalks.... To keep the city safe is a fundamental task of a city's streets and its sidewalks."

JANE JACOBS
The Death and Life of Great American Cities

"…we shall see the imagination build 'walls' of impalpable shadows, comfort itself with the illusion of protection—or, just the contrary: tremble behind thick walls, mistrust the staunchest ramparts."

GASTON BACHELARD
The Poetics of Space

BEFORE AND AFTER VIEWS OF Forest Park (below), St. Louis, and College Homes (facing page), Knoxville, Tennessee. In areas marred by vacant lots and empty streets, these proposals seek to restore the types of lively urban spaces that reinforce a sense of security.

this is a managed environment, "owned" by the neighbors who live there, and under control.

The principles that apply for residential streets of all scales—those lined with small cottages and with high-rise apartment buildings—share the following qualities. The formal fronts of houses face each other across the street as if in polite conversation, creating a congenial, shared address for residents and a courteous welcome for passersby. All visible facades have large windows. Front yards are defined with low plantings or fences, and if there are porches, they are open and dignified. Back yards, garages, and service areas are screened from the public by the houses themselves. (Every blank wall, high fence, or garage door facing the street weakens the relationship between the house and the street and its residents' ability to maintain security.) House facades are in scale with the width of the street to create a room-like quality that enhances the sense of community and conviviality.

COMMERCIAL STREETS

Streets that feel safe and secure are lined with glass-windowed storefronts that display wares and provide views between the interior of the shops and the street. Merchants keep their eyes on street activity, looking for customers and making sure all is well.

The principles that apply include the following: The edge of the public right-of-way is lined with continuous shopfronts—at least 50 percent with transparent facades—that face each other across the street. Ample sidewalks, with landscape treatments and effective lighting, provide a place for chance encounters. Parking is on the street, and the scale of the architecture creates a pleasant, room-like environment. Service and storage facilities are hidden behind the buildings in alleys to avoid blank walls, garage doors, or hidden corners. Where buildings are interrupted for parking areas, streets provide clear, open views of shops and parking spaces, while continuing the landscaping, street trees, and other design treatments. Windows that allow surveillance from the offices and apartments of upper floors contribute to our comfort.

"The goal of the city is to
make man happy and safe."
ARISTOTLE

CIVIC SPACE

Large-scale civic boulevards, parks, and squares lined
with monumental buildings make us comfortable
even though the buildings have fewer direct openings
onto the public space than either neighborhood
streets or commercial streets.

The principles that apply include the following:
The scale of the civic space is large enough, and
the vistas broad enough, that all parts can be seen
by people in the space and by motorists driving
through. Entrances to the buildings are clearly
marked. There is ample and regular lighting. Trees
and landscape materials do not block views at
eye level. The sizes of buildings are in scale with
the dimensions of the space to communicate its
importance. As many windows as possible look
out onto the space.

Traditional building types and spaces offer
more than architectural form; they also coincide
with how our society works. If we follow traditional principles of public and private domain—
front yard, back yard, correct design of streets to
promote neighborliness and discourage through
traffic—we will avoid trouble. In general, you
will find opportunities for crime—or at least the
perception of being unsafe—where these basic
principles have been violated.

RAY GINDROZ
Ray Gindroz is a founding principal and architect with Urban Design Associates (UDA) in
Pittsburgh. Among the numerous inner-city neighborhoods he has designed are those that have
rehabilitated public housing projects. He formerly taught urban design at Yale. He is a board
member of CNU and former chair of CNU's Inner City Task Force.

The Rebirth of Bryant Park

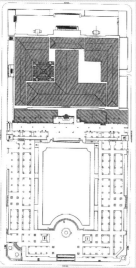

New York City's Bryant Park is a spectacularly safe and sought-after urban park. But 20 years ago, six-acre Bryant Park—the only open space at the heart of midtown Manhattan's 26 million square feet of offices and shops stuffed into the world's greatest collection of skyscrapers—was a heart of darkness. During the previous decade it had become "needle park"—dominated by drug dealers, dreaded by the public, the scene of two murders and at least one other felony every three days.

Decline and degradation were not the end of the Bryant Park story, but the beginning of a night-into-day transformation. A partnership composed of the city, a foundation, building owners around the park, and a nonprofit park restoration group spent $9 million on a comprehensive two-year overhaul. Seven years later, Bryant Park is probably the most sought-after public space in New York—at once midtown's front lawn and its living room carpet. The park regularly draws lunchtime crowds of 10,000. Mothers and toddlers smell the flowers. Orange-robed Tibetan Buddhist monks munch sandwiches and gaze at the top of the Empire State Building. Shirt-sleeved businessmen and women sit in circles on the great lawn to continue meetings that began indoors. On summer nights, as many as 11,000 people gather to view classic movies on a giant screen.

Drug dealers disappeared the day the park reopened in 1992 and have never returned. Crime is practically nonexistent: Two of the first 4 million visitors to the restored park have had their pockets picked. What went right? Restorers rejected the idea that the park could solve its safety problems by restricting access. Instead, a study by the late William H. Whyte, the great modern student of public spaces, disclosed that long before drug dealers made it dangerous, the park had been chronically under-used for almost half a century, because of fatal flaws in its 1934 design as a secluded, formal French garden.

As a result, Bryant Park had always been psychologically unsafe—a place where fearfulness had a stronger hold than delight. The park had been surrounded by a series of high hedges, so that people on the street had no way of knowing what was inside, pleasant or unpleasant. People who did venture in felt trapped in a maze. There were not nearly enough entrances and exits, and the few that existed had steep, narrow steps.

The new park, hedge-free and awash with entrances, entices people with restaurants and handsomely labeled food kiosks, 2,000 movable, green folding chairs, opulent flower beds, nonstop security patrols, restrooms with fresh flowers and baby-changing stations, and a full-time cleaning staff that daily removes more than a ton of trash. Bryant Park is almost self-supporting: Concessions and neighboring landlords cover 90 percent of its $2.5 million annual operating budget, and the park simultaneously subsidizes the owners of nearby buildings. Rents in the area have gone up by as much as 100 percent.

—TONY HISS

TONY HISS

Tony Hiss is the author of numerous books, including *The Experience of Place.*

TWENTY YEARS AGO, BRYANT PARK in midtown Manhattan was a heart of darkness. By correcting decades-old design flaws that invited nefarious activities, the park renovation of 1992 created a safe and inviting urban space.

Twenty two

In the contemporary metropolis, development must adequately accommodate automobiles. It should do so in ways that respect the pedestrian and the form of public space.

DOUGLAS FARR

Automobiles are a fact of modern life, and they are not going away. Walking, on the other hand, faces extinction in most places built since World War II—places designed for the convenient use of cars. This is nothing new, since the forms of cities and towns have always adapted to people's dominant method of getting around. What is different is that places designed around cars are hostile to pedestrians. Try to walk across an eight-lane suburban arterial, and you understand this immediately.

For thousands of years, urban streets and spaces accommodated the flow of pedestrians and domesticated animals. When humans hitched wagons to animals, urban development adapted to the size of the rigs and the room they needed to maneuver. American cities of the 19th century were laid out for horse-drawn vehicles. At first, the auto seemed to fit in nicely. The first autos were more maneuverable, smaller, and fewer in number than the horse-drawn carriage rigs, and they had little effect on city planning.

Enter the Automobile Age, and all hell breaks loose. Automobile ownership grows exponentially, setting several forces in motion. A design manifesto called the Athens Charter, written by Le Corbusier and other leading Modern architects in 1943, advocates designing places around cars. Zoning and building codes are promulgated making it illegal to do anything but to design for cars. Some architects forget how to design pedestrian-friendly public places. People cease to value public spaces.

ACROSS THE COUNTRY, both pedestrian malls and interior malls are dying. This illustrates the paradox of modern retail development. Too many cars scare away pedestrians, while too few starve the retailers. Mizner Park, in Boca Raton, Florida (left), strikes a balance by replacing a dead mall with a mixed-use community facing a revived street.

"In Houston, a person
walking is somebody
on the way to their car."
ANTHONY DOWNS

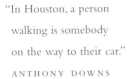

"[S]treets require and use
vast amounts of land.
In the United States, 25
to 35 percent of a city's
developed land is likely
to be in public right-of-
way, mostly in streets....
If we can develop and
design streets so they are
wonderful, fulfilling places
to be... then we will
have successfully designed
about one-third of the
city directly and will have
an immense impact on
the rest."

ALLAN B. JACOBS
Great Streets

What remains is a tragic paradox: a metropolitan region where cars can travel anywhere while pedestrians cannot. The importance of this Charter principle emerges when one understands that when places are designed exclusively for cars, fewer people will walk.

We Americans love our freedoms, and the automobile gave us the freedom not to walk much. Judging by the record numbers of obese Americans, we are enthusiastically exercising our freedom not to walk. We also love convenience. People will drive rather than walk even incredibly short distances if parking is convenient at both ends of the trip. Once in a car, people find it convenient to make all trips in a car, whether cross-town or down the block. This results in ever-increasing numbers of trips by car and total miles driven—a 30 percent increase in vehicle miles traveled (VMT) since 1989 alone. We need a national "12-step" program to get and keep people out of their cars.

At the same time, we need to be realistic. Most people will continue to drive their cars, so streets must oblige traffic. But we need better streets and public spaces than most new ones being built. They must be reasonably pleasant and convenient for motoring, but delightful for walking and cycling. The addition of bike lanes, sidewalks, and trees to facilitate people-powered transit also has the benefit of making the street narrower, so drivers tend to slow down.

A first step would be to give architects and urban designers a remedial education on how to make good multi-purpose public streets. The design elements that contribute to success vary, but several universal design principles emerge.

PROTECT THE PEDESTRIAN

Start with providing sidewalks. Not surprisingly, people walk more when there are sidewalks and less if they are forced to walk in a street or a ditch. Second, reduce traffic speeds to increase pedestrian safety. Traffic engineers will tell you that driving speeds are largely determined by street width and the number of lanes; posted speed limits are meaningless. Drivers will ignore a 25-mile-an-hour sign on an eight-lane arterial. Conversely, it feels risky to drive faster than 30 on a narrow street with cars parked on both sides.

Traffic circles and other "traffic-calming" tools can reduce vehicle speeds and foster a safe pedestrian environment (above left). Drivers sometimes protest when such measures are installed, but it turns out they can improve traffic flow on a street. Traffic circles can be particularly effective because they allow traffic to flow without stopping, whereas stop-lights and four-way stops can generate more air and noise pollution. What enhances safety for pedestrians makes driving safer, too. In 1998, the city of Seattle reported that the installation of 119 traffic-calming projects reduced accidents by 94 percent at those locations.

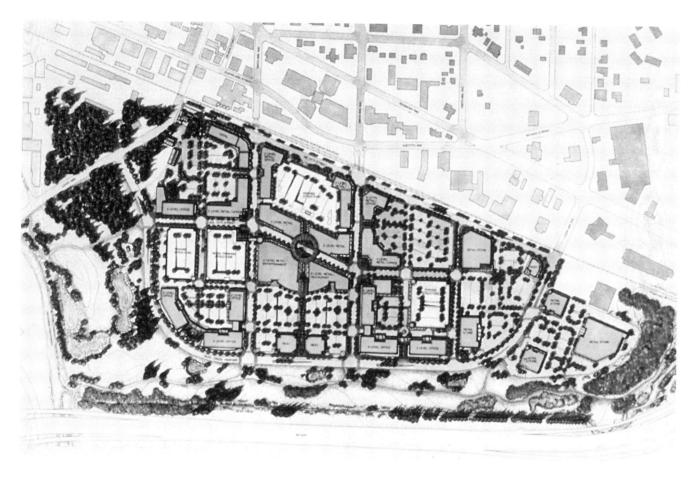

IN REDMOND, WASHINGTON, a mall is being reconstructed as Redmond Town Center, a "Main Street"–style development that includes a traditional street grid. The 120-acre site works for both pedestrians and autos because it combines walkable, shaded streets, urban density, and nearby parking spaces located behind buildings.

BE SMART ABOUT PARKING

Americans expect to drive everywhere and park free. Suburban malls and big-box retailers create such expectations by routinely providing huge parking lots—big enough for the Friday after Thanksgiving rush (sometimes called "Black Friday"), the biggest shopping day of the year. The real-estate industry is convinced that people will not walk more than 300 feet (a 70-second walk) from their car to the mall. But the large surface parking lots in most suburban areas create harsh environments that discourage people from walking even across the street.

One successful design strategy is to move storefronts flush to the street and to locate the off-street parking out of the way. *The Pedestrian Pocket Book: A New Suburban Design Strategy* (Princeton Architectural Press, 1989), edited by Douglas Kelbaugh, illustrates these choices well. In Washington state, new regional malls are being built on a gridded street system with parking structures instead of vast parking lots. This places storefronts on the street in a manner similar to the traditional Main Street, but with the convenient parking and

big-box shopping you expect to find in the suburbs. Due to the differing hours of their use, movie theaters and shops can share this parking. In addition, the parking structures (above) can be designed to look and function like "real" buildings complete with brick facades and ground-floor shops.

In downtown and infill sites where walking and public transportation are viable, the number of parking spaces can be greatly reduced. In Denver, the 50,000-seat Coors Field, built in 1995, required the construction of only 4,600 new parking spaces because planners took into account the 44,000 existing spaces within a 15-minute walk. Instead of being engulfed by parking, the stadium is surrounded by popular bars, galleries, and restaurants, and a thriving loft and apartment scene in the Lower Downtown Historic District. Toronto's 50,000-seat SkyDome baseball stadium was built with no new parking since it sits at the hub of the public transit system and is right next to the central business and entertainment districts.

PEDESTRIANS NEED STIMULATION (below) and are put off by dead spaces like parking lots. A parking garage (above) that functions like a building on the ground floor contributes to a lively streetscape.

STRIKE A BALANCE

Pedestrian malls built across America in the 1960s and 1970s are now being dismantled because storefront businesses located on public streets seem to need automobile traffic to thrive. Here's another paradox. Too many cars on a street scare away the pedestrians, while too few cars starve the retailers. For designers of streets and public spaces, this premise underscores the modern-day interdependence between pedestrians and automobiles.

Chicago's legendary State Street (right) was recently converted from a diesel exhaust–dominated bus mall back into a full-use auto street. The sidewalks were carefully designed to screen pedestrians from autos. After years of slow decline, the storefronts along State Street are now 100 percent rented. Upper floors of buildings have been converted to live–work lofts. With the addition of some cars, the street now teems with pedestrians.

Too often we vilify the car without acknowledging its central place in our culture. When we shape our investments in automobile infrastructure more carefully, we can reclaim public spaces in cities while designing new communities that celebrate the pedestrian as well as the automobile.

AFTER A FAILED BUS MALL WAS REMOVED, Chicago's State Street began thriving again as a street shared by autos and pedestrians.

DOUGLAS FARR

Douglas Farr, AIA, is a founding principal of Farr Associates, a Chicago-based architecture and urban design firm. He serves on CNU's environment task force.

EVEN THE MOST MUNDANE STREET can be improved by the addition of
"encroaching elements," as illustrated in this before-and-after view. Encroaching
elements include arcades, canopies, and street trees. They reduce the need for parking
lots, slow traffic speed, and provide "armor" for the sidewalks, making pedestrians
feel safer.

Twenty three

Streets and squares should be safe, comfortable, and interesting to the pedestrian. Properly configured, they encourage walking and enable neighbors to know each other and protect their communities.

V I C T O R D O V E R

An elderly woman in Bluffton, South Carolina, once told me she likes to take her daily walk along a narrow street in the old town, where the homes are lined up closely along the street. She sensed that if she fell or became ill, she could call out to neighbors for help. The street design extended her independence, encouraged her to exercise, and cemented her daily relationships.

Our society once created many different types of streets. A street, lane, boulevard, or parkway was not just a conduit for cars and trolleys, but also a place for socializing, games, commerce, and for civic art.

In this century, we've separated the design of buildings and streets into unrelated tasks. Architects began to view the street, with its traffic, noise, and connection to a larger world beyond their control, as oppressive. Buildings were no longer placed within a street or even in relation to landscapes. They were set back behind large plazas, elevated on giant pedestals, and sometimes connected to each other by climate-controlled "skywalks" high above the street. Meanwhile, road engineering began promoting unimpeded motoring while paying scant attention to pedestrians. The rich palette of street types was replaced by a few standard road designs, each dangerously calibrated for speedy travel and minimal driving skills.

Not surprisingly, planners and designers worked even harder to separate buildings and their outdoor spaces from the hostile street. They began to sink plazas below grade

GARAGE-FRONTED
STREETS lack the surveil-
lance effect provided by
streets with porches, entries,
and windows.

"In general the conception
of the private inside
becomes manifest in the
'threshold' or boundary
which separates it from and
unifies it with the outside.
At the same time the
boundary gives the public
outside its particular
presence. Thus Louis Kahn
says: 'The street is a room
of agreement. The street
is dedicated by each house
owner to the city.' . . .
But the public outside is
something more than an
'agreement' of individual
homes. The agreement
it represents is focused
in public buildings which
concretize the shared
understanding which
makes communal life
possible and meaningful."
CHRISTIAN
NORBERG-SCHULZ
Genius Loci

or to design entire projects with no sidewalks. In cities and suburbs alike, streets became more barren and inhospitable. Elements normally placed to the rear or sides of buildings—like garage doors and parking—began to face the street (above). The architecture turned its back upon the street, with tragic physical results.

That massive cultural experiment has largely ended. Many new developments and redevelopments now showcase the street instead of withdrawing from it. This indicates a larger shift in design and marketing to emphasize community rather than isolation. But how can we regain the ability to create these types of places on a much broader scale? The answer is that it's time to reunite architecture and the creation of public spaces into complementary and seamless tasks.

The details of the right-of-way and the design of adjacent buildings should work together to comfort, satisfy, and stimulate pedestrians. People will walk through areas where they are provided with precise orientation, visual stimulation, protection against the elements, and a variety of activities. Moreover, they must feel safe—both from fear of crime and from fear of being hit by a vehicle.

PLANNING AND DESIGNING WALKABLE COMMERCIAL AREAS

People walk more when the streets connect destinations along logical routes. Planning for the pedestrian begins with the creation of an interconnected network of streets, midblock passages, alleys, pocket parks, and trails that provide lots of options for reaching any particular place. This network should direct people toward shops and services, and enhance the sense that walking is more convenient than driving and parking. Blocks should be small, so pedestrians can get across and around them quickly. The 200-foot-square blocks of Portland, Oregon, are part of what makes the city feel so walkable. So too are the 530 intersections per square mile in central Savannah, Georgia—more crossings than found in central Rome.

The right-of-way details also matter greatly. Sidewalk width, curbs, corner curb radii, lane width, on-street parking, trees, and lighting should encourage the pedestrian's confident movement. On Main Street, sidewalks around 14 feet wide typically work best. On residential streets, provide a tree planting strip at least five feet wide between the curb and the sidewalk. On low-density residential streets, a five-foot-wide "detached" sidewalk suffices. Curbs should be upright, not rounded or "rolled" curb-and-gutter combinations. The "stand-up" curb orders the space and controls the way people drive and park. The stand-up curb also reassures pedestrians that motorists will not leave the roadway and hit them on the sidewalk. Corner curb radii should be as small as practical. The smaller the radius, the shorter the distance pedestrians must walk to cross the street. Motorists navigate turns more carefully when the corner curb radius is small.

On-street parking helps in many ways. Every car stored on the street decreases the demand for land-wasting parking lots. Furthermore, parked cars buffer pedestrians from moving cars. This "armor" effect makes pedestrians comfortable. On-street parking also calms traffic because motorists must be

alert for opening doors and cars entering the road-way. Finally, parking spaces located near storefronts appear to help stores bring in customers.

Street trees usually are an essential building block to create such an environment. They provide shade for pedestrians and buildings, further establish the scale and rhythm of the street, and contribute to slower, more careful driving by making the street feel narrower. The trees should be of a consistent species, spaced regularly, and aligned consistently.

To complement the commercial street, the architectural design of storefronts should incorporate *encroaching elements* (right) to shade interiors and shelter pedestrians (above). Encroaching elements include awnings, arcades, colonnades, and canti-levered balconies. Vernacular architecture always provides variations fine-tuned to local culture, weather, and building technologies. The streets of Istanbul and other Islamic cities are faced by deco-rous *jumbas*, or screened balconies. In response to the tropical sun, colonial cities in the Caribbean feature substantial masonry arcades. The streets of New Orleans feature delicate wrought-iron veran-das. A storefront in Annapolis may have a simple, elegant canvas awning. All these measures moderate the climate while providing the visual interest craved by pedestrians, who quickly tire of walking along parking lots, blank walls, or endless rows of identical anything. Doors and windows facing public space create a safer environment that also engages the pedestrian's interest. On Main Street in particular, many doors along storefronts enliven the street.

DESIGNING SAFE RESIDENTIAL STREETS

A key to neighborhood safety is *natural surveillance*, a crime-prevention term that describes the phe-nomenon in which misbehavior decreases when it looks like there might be someone watching. Again, a combination of sound planning, urban design, street design, and building design is necessary to create such environments. Buildings that face public spaces must include windows, doors, and other outward signs of human occupancy, such as porches and balconies. The would-be miscreant immediately knows this is a watched-over place. Positioning buildings with windows, porches, and balconies close to the street or other public space also creates a "territorial" feel. This promotes a bond among neighbors, who share a sense of ownership of that space. When natural surveillance is in effect, neigh-bors feel empowered to protect their communities and demand responsible behavior.

Mixed uses can create safe neighborhood streets as well. When the entire street consists of a single use (for example, single-family houses), then natural surveillance can drop. In many households, two working parents are now common, so there may be times during the day when no one is around. Conversely, if different types of households are mixed with other uses along the street, the space is more likely to be monitored more times of the day and night.

Traffic safety is another big neighborhood issue. Until recently, road engineers put the safety of motorists first by designing roads and intersections for speeds beyond the posted limit. The idea was to

"Simple as it may be, this relationship of the building to the sidewalk is one of the key architectural deci-sions in city planning for cohesive neighborhoods.... The good news is that the relationship is a very simple one: place the building at the sidewalk. That's it."
DAVID SUCHER
City Comforts

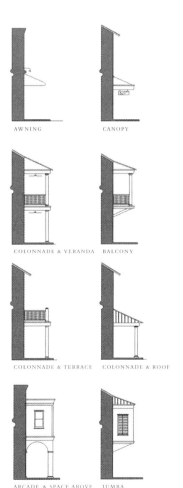

AWNING   CANOPY

COLONNADE & VERANDA   BALCONY

COLONNADE & TERRACE   COLONNADE & ROOF

ARCADE & SPACE ABOVE   JUMBA

"The measure of any great
civilization is its cities and
a measure of a city's great-
ness is to be found in the
quality of its public spaces,
its parks and squares."

JOHN RUSKIN

protect those motorists who drive carelessly or too
fast. But when the road is designed for speeding,
people take advantage of that invitation, and more
mayhem results. Traffic calming reverses this
approach by providing physical cues—including
street trees, narrower streets, traffic circles, and
intersections designed for pedestrians—to slow
down rather than speed up.

SQUARES AND PLAZAS

Our modern urban plazas suffer from many of the
same problems as modern streets. Especially at the
base of high-rise office buildings, they frequently
showcase the building rather than encourage or
shelter the pedestrian. They are indifferent to their
climate and environs, and thus are unpleasant to
walk through or to inhabit. Fortunately, many of
these places can be rescued. In almost every city,
dull urban plazas have already been improved to
provide new seating, shade, and places to eat, shop,
or enjoy performances.

The size and placement of squares should
relate to their purpose and context. Their design
image should be driven by climate, culture, and the
activities likely to occur there. Plazas and squares

should be located where they will be used—near
cafes and storefronts, or in front of a courthouse,
for example—and where they enhance real-estate
value. Regional traditions should inform the choice
between a soft, green space such as the village
common found in small towns in the Northeast
and Midwest, or the paved plaza found in Latin
America, the Caribbean, or the Mediterranean.

For too many years, cities and towns turned
inwards by replacing their shopping streets with
interior malls, supplanting ground-level sidewalks
with enclosed bridges, and placing parking in spots
once inhabited by street-level shops and activities.
Much was lost, but we're discovering we can
integrate the design of architecture and streets
to regain the vigor of public spaces.

VICTOR DOVER

Victor Dover, AICP, is a planner and principal in Dover, Kohl & Partners, Town Planning,
in South Miami, Florida. He is a founding member of CNU.

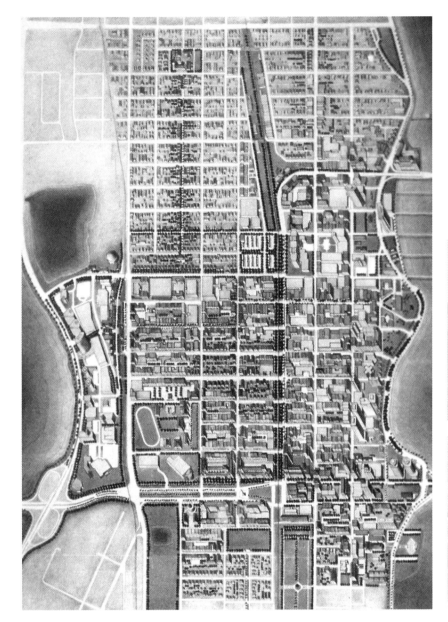

PUBLIC SQUARES AND PLAZAS are being revived in West Palm Beach, Florida.
The Downtown Illustrative Master Plan (above left) enabled city stakeholders to
understand the vision they posited for their community. Clematis Street as it looks
today (bottom) and its proposed renovation (above middle). A new interactive fountain
in front of the library at one end of Clematis Street (top right) supported the revival
of the downtown's main retail street.

The Recovery of the Public Realm

"In a city the street must be supreme. It is the first institution of the city. The street is a room by agreement, a community room, the walls of which belong to the donors, dedicated to the city for common use. Its ceiling is the sky."

LOUIS I. KAHN
Between Silence and Light

The state of this country's public spaces is both exciting and sobering. On the one hand, the past 20 years have produced a magnificent revival of public places. Major sites in central locations—urban riverfronts, downtown plazas and parks, fashionable shopping streets, and historic districts—have been renovated and are better kept than ever before. These places have received lavish public and private investment and been the focus of innovative management efforts that sustain their vitality. As a consequence, they are extremely well used and are brimming with people who go about their business with a freedom and easiness that one rarely encountered in such places just a few years ago.

On the other hand, smaller and less central places—neighborhood streets and parks, playgrounds, gardens, neighborhood squares, and older suburban commercial centers—continue to decline. In fact, many smaller public places have become the victims of redevelopment, privatization, and neglect, and are disappearing altogether. If not addressed, this imbalance will ultimately diminish the rich diversity of the public environment of cities, forever the symbol of our communities' aesthetic and social values. It will also deplete the rich design vocabulary upon which that diversity was built.

A full recovery of both grand and humble public places in cities and older suburbs is in order. Such full recovery, however, requires a rigorous and all-inclusive approach that includes:

- Addressing head-on the forces that contribute to the deterioration of public places. This means managing growth; subordinating private cars to public and other modes of transportation; bringing back the many and integrated civic activities that have fallen out of our lives in the past 50 years; and reversing functional, social, and economic segregation;

- Challenging rules and regulations that inhibit the creation of great public places;

- Thinking creatively of ways to finance and maintain them;

- Looking at each public place as part of a much larger system, in which preserves of wild and rural land are rigorously linked (via greenways and transportation corridors) to the humblest neighborhood places to form a coherent public network of open spaces and pathways;

- Cataloging and understanding the consensual and rich design vocabulary that has given us the elegant and masterly public realm of the past;

- Applying that vocabulary to new places and to the rehabilitation of existing ones, including public and low-income housing;

- Developing and supporting legislation to facilitate the transformation of empty and abandoned lots (including surface parking lots) in neighborhoods and cities into dignified buildings and public places;

- Making citizens partners and ambassadors in the movement to recover public places. It has been through citizen initiatives, after all, that many significant public places and historic buildings have been saved, preserved, or created.

- Focusing on the education of architects and planners. Recovery cannot happen in one generation, and the values and tools to create a successful public realm must be shared and passed along.

Work on the recovery strategies listed above has already started. This is fueled by a growing understanding of how New Urbanist principles apply to older cities and suburbs as much as they do to new development. As a consequence, an increasing number of design professionals employ those principles in their practice. Politicians, developers, bankers, and planners are also paying attention to New Urbanist principles to revisit and rearrange their priorities. Much more, however, remains to be done. Older cities and neighborhoods are complex organisms. A full recovery of the public realm will require many incremental steps and a sustained effort over time. As people who care about our communities and neighborhoods, we have no choice but to continue down this road of recovery, as creating healthy public places is the only way to return brilliance, excitement, and joy to our cities.

—GIANNI LONGO

PUBLIC SPACES ARE UNDERGOING AN EXCITING REVIVAL. Three examples: the lakefront promenade at Laguna West, California (top left); a tot lot (left); and Post Office Square (below), a park built above seven stories of underground parking in downtown Boston. Yet functional parks and open space remain a missing factor from many city and suburban neighborhoods.

GIANNI LONGO

Gianni Longo is a founding principal of American Communities Partnership Visioning and Planning in New York City and is the author of *A Guide to Great American Public Spaces*.

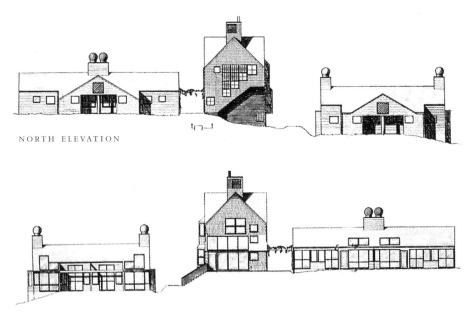

NORTH ELEVATION

SOUTH ELEVATION

PASSIVE SOLAR ARCHITECTURE relies on the orientation of buildings rather than technology. Solar architecture (above) combines south-facing windows, greenhouse walls, and masonry Trombe walls that absorb solar heat and release it into the interior. "Solar chimneys" draw away heat for summer cooling. These and other types of natural heating and ventilation techniques grow from local climate.

Twenty four

Architecture and landscape design should grow from
local climate, topography, history, and building practice.

D O U G L A S   K E L B A U G H

To an urban planner, many New Urbanist principles mean thinking bigger—planning
at the scale of a metropolitan region rather than at the scale of the subdivision. To
an architect or landscape architect, however, this principle means thinking smaller—
resisting the forces that make generic buildings, streets, and blocks, and championing
forces that encourage local design. Also called Regionalism or Critical Regionalism,
this attitude celebrates and delights in what is different about a place.

This principle roots architecture and landscape design in local culture and the
genius loci. It is a reaction against the standardization and homogenization of Modernism,
which typically substituted technological fixes (air conditioning, for example) for
architectural responses to climate, topography, and building practice.

Within this principle's emphasis on climate and topography, the Charter also asserts
the importance of the vertical cycles, loops, and chains of nature. Understanding and
preserving these natural systems is essential to ecological health, as is respect for the land
and its geology, hydrology, biota, and the cyclical processes that nourish and cleanse
the environment.

CLIMATE

The 1970s energy crisis promoted architecture that was more sympathetic to the environment. This ecological view encouraged designers to employ active and passive solar heating and cooling, as well as natural lighting and ventilation, especially in smaller, more climate-responsive buildings.

Most important, this movement compelled many designers and builders to make buildings more site-specific—crafted to the local climate, solar radiation, terrain, building materials, and practices. It has been paralleled in landscape architecture by such movements as Xeriscape—using native and climate-adapted plants that need less water, fertilizer, and pesticides. This is not only a question of conserving BTUs, but also of assuming a more humble view of humanity's place in the natural world. It rejects the single-mindedness that often characterizes engineering solutions for an approach that simultaneously addresses social, environmental, and aesthetic issues.

The "single house" of Charleston (below) provides an excellent historical example of climate-sensitive architecture that creates urbane streetscapes and lush private gardens. The single house features two-story side porches that provide shade and space for outdoor living, as well as high ceilings and tall windows for cross-ventilation. Many houses at Seaside, Florida, include neo-traditional houses with large porches and natural ventilation.

HISTORY

The best blocks, streets, and buildings in American cities are often the historic ones. Witness the surviving colonial areas of Boston, Charleston, and Providence, not to mention the Arts-and-Crafts bungalow neighborhoods of countless cities across North America.

This heritage should be preserved, adapted, and studied for design principles, patterns, and typologies rather than used as a grab bag of styles. Time-tested architectural types are more valuable antecedents than specific historical styles. Whether vernacular or high-style, the finest buildings from the past continue to set the standard of excellence and to act as a treasury of enduring form. Whether uncultivated or formal, the most beautiful landscapes from the past inspire us in the same fashion.

Designers need not continually invent new form. Originality for its own sake is neither better nor less slavish than the superficial copying of other times and places. New Urbanists must respect authentic, living traditions without resorting to empty historical mimicry, just as surely as they reject avant-garde trendiness and naive futurism. When designing blocks, streets, and buildings, New Urbanists should view local precedents and conventions as a point of departure. Conventional design vocabulary and syntax then can be incrementally transformed to express and accommodate new technical innovations and programmatic changes.

Local architectural language can evolve, much as spoken language does in multilingual dialects, and much as new words are coined to name new scientific and technological developments. If it evolves either too slowly or too suddenly, it loses its meaning and power. Change succeeds when it is fresh but not too radical or disorienting, so that it rhymes across time and space.

TOPOGRAPHY

The earth's surface has been denatured by centuries of massive earthmoving that has created wholesale reconfiguration of land. Often the result has been run-off, erosion, and flooding of biblical proportions. From topsoil to treetops, the landscape has been disfigured and violated by the wholesale bulldozing of America (right).

To slow our rapacious consumption of the hinterland, New Urbanism underscores the importance of inscribing a horizontal circle of compact, pedestrian-friendly, mixed-use development on the

land, as exemplified by the concept known as a "pedestrian pocket" (also known as transit-oriented development). To increase vehicular and pedestrian connectivity, New Urbanist projects have revived the grid as a pattern of development and circulation. When overlaid on hilly topography, the grid-iron can result in the types of dramatic streetscapes and views for which San Francisco and Seattle are famous. Even when interrupted by topographic features, the grid provides greater connection within urban circulation patterns than the curvilinear streets of conventional sprawl, which is often naturalistic in superficial and artificial ways.

BUILDING MATERIALS AND TECHNIQUES

The Modernist search for standardized solutions has devolved into the Post-Modernist search for variety. Contemporary modes of production and distribution make this possible. Standardized building components are reverting to customized components, helped along by both the flexibility of computerized manufacturing and the speedy international distribution of goods and services.

In short, designers can now specify any product in any color or style from anywhere in the world. This freedom has not usually resulted in better design. Indeed, one can argue that contemporary buildings, blocks, and neighborhoods have developed too much visual or stylistic variety. They often contain a riot of different building materials, colors, shapes, and motifs that lack coherence or grounding in local building practices. New products

"Now that we have built the sprawling system of far-flung houses, offices, and discount marts connected by freeways, we can't afford to live in it. We also failed to anticipate the costs of the social problems we created in letting our towns and cities go to hell. Two generations have grown up and matured in America without experiencing what it is like to live in a human habitat of quality. We have lost so much culture in the sense of how to build things well. Bodies of knowledge and sets of skills that took centuries to develop were tossed into the garbage, and we will not get them back easily. The culture of architecture was lost to Modernism and its dogmas. The culture of town planning was handed over to lawyers and bureaucrats, with pockets of resistance mopped up by the automobile, highway, and real estate interests."

JAMES HOWARD KUNSTLER
The Geography of Nowhere

THE PEDESTRIAN POCKET (below), also known as transit-oriented development, combines strategies for mixed-use development, transit, and walkability. When this rational diagram is applied to a real piece of land, it must be adjusted to inflect local history, topography, and circumstance.

are vended at a rate that makes it difficult if not impossible for users to evaluate them, or for knowledge to accumulate in meaningful ways.

The size of contemporary residential and commercial projects has increased enormously, resulting in two different but equally problematic design strategies. One introduces a false diversity of materials, textures, color, and style. The other rigidly controls these variables. In the former case, tectonic integrity is usually lost. Only rarely can a single design team or building contractor master multiple architectural languages and styles, each of which uses different materials in different ways. In the latter case, a limited palette of materials and

colors results in tedious repetition and lifeless uniformity. Neither strategy seems to produce the design integrity or richness of local, incremental development, where the hand and human touch of individual builders and designers is more evident. Variations and reinterpretations of local architectural types, especially when constructed with local building materials, produces more genuine diversity than either polyglot diversity or uniform design controls.

The loss of local building knowledge and traditions has been accompanied by a precipitous decline in the quality of contemporary building construction. The sheetrocking of America occurred

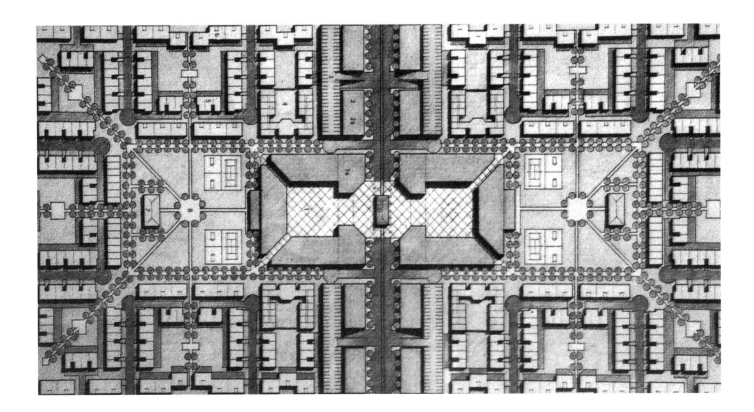

in a single lifetime. Buildings became more like stage sets, unable to take a kick or even a punch from a vandal. Ersatz and fake materials that imitate nobler materials have existed throughout the history of building and architecture. Colonial buildings disguised wood as stone, and the Victorians fooled the eye with pressed tin and prefab cast-iron facades. But tectonic impersonation and scenographic construction have worsened with commercial image-making, as well as with the shorter and shorter life spans of contemporary buildings.

As a result of this impoverishment of the built environment, more people seek more permanent materials and better craftsmanship. Environmentally aware consumers also demand local and recycled materials as well as other "green" products, which save on transportation costs, clean-up, and embodied energy.

In the increasingly global cultures of trade, tourism, and telecommunications, it has become essential to recognize and defend local differences in climate, topography, history, and building practice. Authenticity commands a higher, not a lower, premium in a more highly mediated world. In the end, architecture and landscape design are not words or paper but buildings and their surrounds. Situated in microclimates, on the ground, connecting past to the future, palpably there, alive with flora and fauna, they are the stage for life itself.

"There are global economic and cultural forces that turn all architecture— modern, traditional, and Post-Modern—into a commodity that merely adorns an increasingly degraded environment."
ALAN PLATTUS
Associate Dean,
School of Architecture,
Yale University

DOUGLAS KELBAUGH

Douglas Kelbaugh, FAIA, is dean of the College of Architecture and Urban Planning at the University of Michigan. A pioneer of passive solar design, he has received many awards for his architecture and urban design projects. He is the editor of *The Pedestrian Pocket Book: A New Suburban Design Strategy* (Princeton Architectural Press, 1989) and author of *Common Place: Toward Neighborhood and Regional Design* (University of Washington Press, 1997).

IN TRADITIONAL TOWNS, public buildings stand out from ordinary residences and shops in design and scale. Today this relationship is frequently reversed. Indeed, citizens would be surprised if their local post office were as well built as a new restaurant, if the town hall were as fine as a department store.

Twenty five

Civic buildings and public gathering places require important sites to reinforce community identity and the culture of democracy. They deserve distinctive form, because their role is different from that of other buildings and places that constitute the fabric of the city.

ANDRES DUANY

It is surely one of the minor mysteries of modern times that civic buildings in America have become cheap to the point of squalor when they were once quite magnificent as a matter of course. Our post offices, public schools and colleges, fire stations, town halls, and all the rest are no longer honored with an architecture of fine materials, tall spaces, and grandeur of form. The new civic buildings are useful enough, but they are incapable of providing identity or pride for their communities.

Today's civic buildings tend to be less accomplished even than run-of-the-mill commercial structures. Indeed, citizens would be surprised if their local post office were as well built as a new restaurant, if the town hall were as fine as a department store, or the community college as grand as a regional shopping mall.

This inversion in the civic and private hierarchy has no precedent in American society and is alien to the sensibility of most cultures. Why should this sad situation be uniquely ours? Surely this nation is wealthier than it has ever been. As late as the 1950s, civic structures were still the best buildings in town.

At the heart of the change is the definition of infrastructure. Infrastructure is the supporting armature of urbanism. Today's definition is constrained by utilitarian thinking. It includes only thoroughfares and utilities. Indeed the term *infrastructure* is a neologism including the technical while excluding the civic.

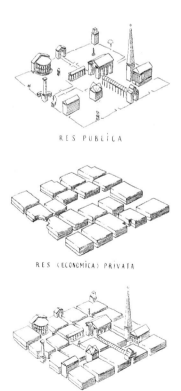

RES PUBLICA

RES (ECONOMICA) PRIVATA

CIVITAS

"Participation in the *res publica* today is most often a matter of going along, and the forums for this public life, like the city, are in a state of decay."

RICHARD SENNETT
The Fall of Public Man

Civic buildings were once included with thoroughfares and utilities in the term *public works.* Voters could decide with equanimity between, say, a school *or* a road. Given the choice they would often fund the civic building. After all, civic buildings are the *social* infrastructure, no less important than the *movement* infrastructure of vehicles, fluids, and power.

The postwar process by which urban planning became a collection of specialties destroyed the unified conception of public works and, as with so much else in planning, a bias for the technical prevailed. Investment in roads now receives the dedicated gasoline tax, but civic buildings must be "subsidized" from other sources. And in the case of cultural buildings like museums, these sources are reduced to random private benefactors.

The United States, where roads are repaired sooner than schools, thus boasts of the world's best infrastructure and the civic buildings of an underdeveloped country. Only if horizontal and vertical infrastructure are joined again as public works can there be an intelligent, indeed democratic, allocation of available resources.

Public buildings are those sponsored exclusively by government: the city halls, town halls, armories, transportation and postal facilities, public schools and colleges, as well as the few cultural facilities of national importance, such as the Smithsonian. However, many equally important communal organizations such as the Metropolitan Museum and the Boston Symphony are funded privately. These belong to the civic category.

Civic buildings may receive government sponsorship, but they are administered by nonprofit groups. The distinction between the civic and the public is not particularly important in America, where government prefers to confine its investment to public infrastructure and private nonprofits must compensate.

Private clubs that do not receive government subsidy, but nevertheless perform a communal function, should too be considered civic. And, not entirely outside of this category, are the many places that play a communal role while belonging neither to the civic nor the public categories. These are the common, informal daily gathering places between the poles of workplace and residence. They are typically diners, corner stores, cafes, rathskellers, pubs, barber shops, hotel lobbies, and the like categorized as "third places" by Ray Oldenburg in *The Great Good Place*.

Within a new community, public and civic buildings will come into being as the urbanism evolves, but only if some provision is made for them early in the planning process. To overcome the innate resistance to public expenditure, the master plan can reserve lots for generic civic buildings. The type of building is left to be determined by the society eventually. In the early phases of build-out, civic investment may seem utopian, but citizens of a successful place will eventually want to endow themselves with culture, and to embellish their beloved community with civic buildings. Evidence of these sentiments can be seen in every

great American city and many towns. The availability of a site acts as a constant reminder that in itself may well catalyze the civic institution.

The natural evolution of civic buildings, however, cannot occur within private community associations as currently conceived. These are structured to achieve stasis, to avoid deterioration, but consequently making impossible improvements to the community. These associations are enabled to collect normal dues for maintenance and even for periodic reconstruction of infrastructure, but not for the kind of investment that creates civic facilities. But the articles of association can easily incorporate this important role by providing for a small, dedicated, and permanent tax. This trickle of funds will accumulate for a periodic civic improvement.

Another promising strategy is currently evolving. Studies by the Bay Area marketing firm American Lives have identified certain civic buildings that the buyers prefer to the "amenities" commonly provided by developers. These amenities are usually golf courses, guarded entries, club houses, and other costly items included primarily for marketing purposes. The new studies have determined that an amenity such as a small library is considered more desirable than one of the elaborate, guarded "entry features" at approximately the same cost. For most developments, such budget allocations are normal, and it is only a matter of slightly altering standard practice to fund authentic civic buildings from the outset of the construction of the community.

As a consequence of the demise of the concept of public works, once the horizontal infrastructure is built there may not be much budget remaining for civic buildings. Consequently they are often smaller than the private buildings that surround them. But there are ways to overcome this problem. Reserving a location at the termination of an axis can powerfully enhance the importance of a building. It is remarkable how even a rudimentary building (such as a fire station housed in a prefabricated metal structure) gains in importance and dignity when it sits squarely at the end of an avenue or within a square. To waste such sites on private buildings is a cultural loss.

Another, more subtle way to enhance a civic building is recommended by Leon Krier. Since terminated axes are not often available, he would reserve the classical language (columns, pediments, and all the rest) for civic buildings, with the private

"Public space and monumental architecture are like precious jewelry. Too much of it is a false luxury. Too little of it is a false economy. The good city can only be made of streets and squares. The square, a most natural place of convention, is the choice location of all things public, of *res publica* and its noblest expression: monumental architecture."
LEON KRIER

"Twentieth-century America has seen a steady, persistent decline in the visual and emotional power of its public buildings, and this has been accompanied by a not less persistent decline in the authority of public order."
DANIEL PATRICK MOYNIHAN

DOOLITTLE MAP OF 1824

New Haven, Connecticut

TODAY'S PUBLIC
BUILDINGS can express
community pride by being
placed on a special site,
such as the New Haven
Green (above). Catalog of
types of public squares that
can contain public buildings
(below). In such a setting,
even a rudimentary pre-
fab metal structure would
attain dignity.

buildings remaining in the common or vernacular
language. This dialectic of classical and vernacular
taps into deep cultural and perhaps even physio-
logical roots. This effect can be experienced in
the Lyceum in Alexandria, Virginia. The Lyceum
is a small classical building that establishes its
precedence although it is much smaller than the
rowhouses around it.

At the very least there should be an architectural code limiting the private buildings to tectonic
modesty (a visual silence), while the public buildings
are allowed to remain uncoded, thus able to be fully
expressive of the aspirations of the institutions they
embody or, less interestingly, the inspirations of
their architects.

Another technique to characterize an otherwise undistinguished civic building is to place it
within a site developed in an exceptional manner.
This is called the entourage. The simplest entourage
consists of setting the building farther back from
the common building line of the street, creating a
forecourt. A more elaborate strategy is to surround
the civic building with yards that are formally landscaped and equipped with fountains, benches, or
streetlights superior to the standard. This was a preferred device of the City Beautiful movement,
which was responsible for much of what is successfully civic in cities today.

The concentration of civic buildings has
ancient roots. In the Hispanic settlements of the

STANDARD SQUARE   ATTACHED SQUARE   AXIAL SQUARE   DOUBLE AXIAL SQUARE

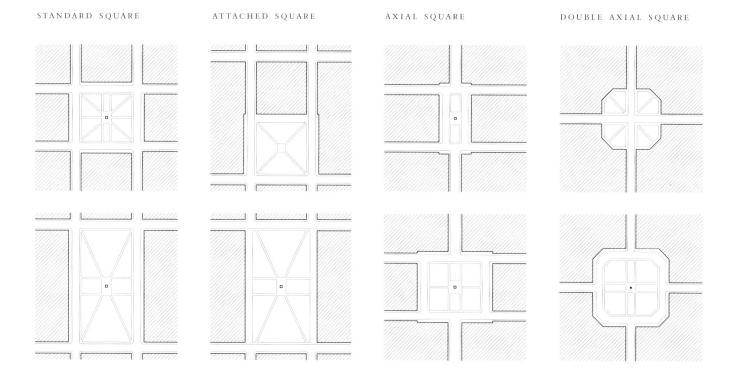

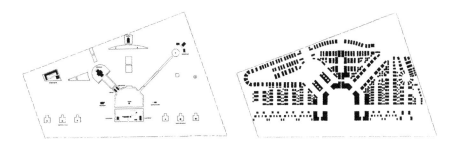

PUBLIC BUILDINGS AND SQUARES CAN BE DISTRIBUTED throughout a neighborhood. Civic buildings, planned in coordination with public open spaces, should be prominently sited, ideally terminating vistas and enclosing streets to serve as landmarks.

Southwest, the church, city hall, and other government buildings were located around the central plaza. This layout resulted from a code called the Law of the Indies. The practice is less consistent in the early New England settlements, but not unknown. A particularly well-known example is in New Haven, where three churches sit on the green, while the library, city hall, and Yale University share the edges. This works well, as it tends to concentrate pedestrians.

The alternative of dispersing the civic buildings throughout the community also has positive secondary effects. The common disparagement of suburban housing as "cookie cutter" may even be overcome. This term refers not merely to monotony, but to the greater problem of disorientation, which cannot be effectively relieved by varying the architectural style of the buildings. It can only be positively affected by the provision of what Kevin Lynch called *landmarks*. Although these vary, and may even include natural features, the landmark most securely under the control of the planner is the allocation of sites for civic buildings. Such buildings are intrinsically different and therefore memorable.

Utilitarian analysis, however, has led to policies that discourage the interspersing of civic buildings throughout the community. For example, in Baton Rouge, Louisiana, the courthouse, the city hall, and much of the bureaucracy reside within a single high-rise called the Government Services Building. Even the mayor's office within is difficult to identify. The entire building looks bureaucratic and provides little civic pride.

This way of thinking is even more devastating when applied to schools. Efficiency of administration does not yield what is best for the students or for the community. It leads only to very large centralized schools. To deprive neighborhoods of small schools that also act as local civic centers is a great loss. But, as expected in a democracy, where mistakes are not avoided but eventually corrected, the movement to smaller, community-based schools is expanding.

If a community is to be successful in the long run—and all planning is for the long run—it is essential that sites be reserved for such schools in every neighborhood. Such is the duty of the planner toward the most important of the civic buildings.

"[H]as there ever been another place on earth where so many people of wealth and power have paid for and put up with so much architecture they detested…? I doubt it seriously. Every child goes to school in a building that looks like a duplicating-machine replacement-parts wholesale distribution warehouse. Not even the school commissioners, who commissioned it and approved the plans, can figure it out. The main thing is to try to avoid having to explain it to the parents."

TOM WOLFE
From Bauhaus to Our House

ANDRES DUANY

Andres Duany is the partner of Elizabeth Plater-Zyberk. Their firm, Duany Plater-Zyberk & Company, has prepared more than 100 new towns and urban revitalization plans. He was among the founders of CNU.

Civic Buildings as Vertical Infrastructure

Civic buildings and spaces should be considered vertical infrastructure. They are long-term investments, as important to the functioning and the welfare of a community as the horizontal infrastructure of thoroughfares and utilities. Together, vertical and horizontal infrastructure should be considered public works.

DEFINING CIVIC AND PUBLIC

Public denotes those buildings and places that the entire community holds in common ownership. They usually pertain to government, public education, recreation, and transportation. Civic is a more comprehensive category, adding to the public facilities those administered by private organizations which provide communal benefit. These are usually religious, cultural, and educational institutions, as well as certain sporting venues.

ENABLING THE CONSTRUCTION OF CIVIC BUILDINGS

Civic places will come into being only if provision is made for them in the urban planning process. It is fundamental that sites be reserved early and made available to suitable organizations. By being conceived as public works, the construction of the buildings may even be financed by the budget residual from the more economical horizontal infrastructure resulting from compact development. Such civic buildings may play the role of amenities that developers deem necessary for marketing purposes. They can substitute for the typical "entry feature" or the golf course.

Another method to fund civic improvements is to tap into the taxation stream of the increasingly common community associations. These can be structured to enable civic improvements in addition to the usual provisions for maintenance.

ON THE PHYSICAL IDENTITY OF CIVIC BUILDINGS

A civic building can be an effective repository of a community's pride and a manifestation of its identity. To do so, the civic building must be readily identifiable as such. It is, however, no longer possible to depend on an identity based on scale, as civic buildings today are often smaller than private ones. A more realistic strategy is to enhance the building by granting it a significant location. Significant sites are generally those that terminate the axial vista of a thoroughfare, or those that enfront or occupy a public open space, such as a plaza or a square. Also, a special landscape associated with the building (the entourage) can create the significant difference.

A supplementary method is to differentiate a civic building by the tectonic elaboration of its construction. This establishes a dialectic between private and civic architecture. This may include the incorporation of an exceptional element such as a tower or a colonnade. Another more subtle method is to reserve certain colors for public buildings, as civic buildings in New England villages are often white clapboard while common buildings are of grey shingle. There is also the recourse to the duality of the timeless classical and vernacular languages.

ON THE CONCENTRATION OR DISPERSION OF CIVIC BUILDINGS

Civic buildings may be concentrated in one place or dispersed throughout the community. There is no question that urbanistically, if not administratively, several smaller public buildings in a campus setting are superior to the single, composite megastructure currently in favor. By separating the program into multiple buildings, the institution's roles are easier to decipher. This is also more likely to decant activity into the public space, rather than internalizing it within a corridor system.

Advice on the wide dispersal of such buildings throughout the community or their concentration at the core is less conclusive. To group all the public buildings does enliven public life at that one place more intensely. On the other hand, the dispersal of these special buildings more equitably leavens the overall fabric of the community and contributes to localized identity. Both have valid precedent in the American urban tradition.

—ANDRES DUANY

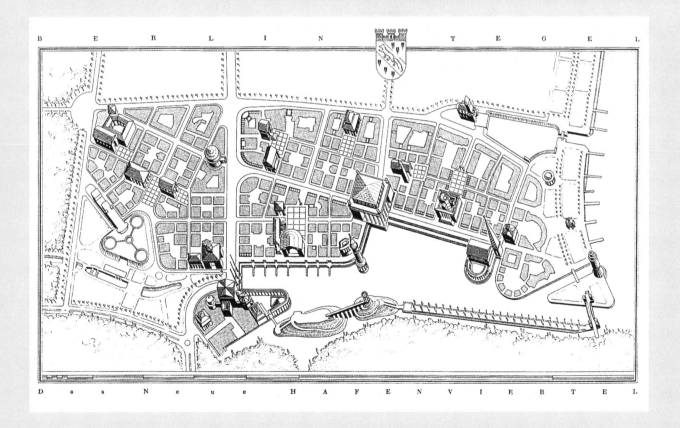

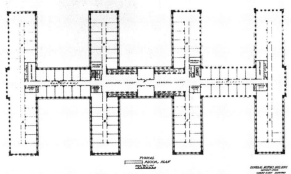

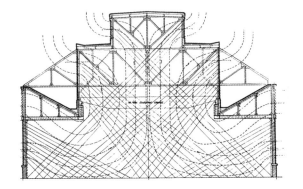

ALBERT KAHN'S General Motors Headquarters (above), built in 1921, placed each worker within 20 feet of an operable window. Kahn's factory buildings, like the Packard Motor Car Company Forge Shop (right), 1911, used extensive glazing and ingenious clerestory systems to bathe factory workers in daylight and to ventilate with little mechanical assistance. The section of the plant shows paths of light and air circulation.

Twenty six

All buildings should provide their inhabitants with a clear sense of location, weather, and time. Natural methods of heating and cooling can be more resource-efficient than mechanical systems.

MARK M. SCHIMMENTI

This Charter principle addresses the issue of a building occupant's awareness of and connection to the outside world. All buildings should be designed so that people live and work close to operable windows, to provide access to natural light and air, and to reduce the reliance on energy-hungry climate control systems.

Buildings that isolate people from the environment are antithetical to this principle. Most new, nonresidential structures have either vast areas separated from windows or no windows at all. Many building types—grocery stores, office buildings, factories, and especially "big-box" commercial stores—have evolved into windowless boxes. Sealed off from the outside world, such buildings isolate their occupants from a sense of location, weather, and time, and must rely completely on mechanical systems for temperature control, ventilation, and artificial sources of light.

Until recently, almost all building types fostered a strong relationship between the inside and the outside. The American front porch is an icon of the house's relationship to the outside world of the street and neighborhood. School classrooms had large windows and courtyards. Albert Kahn's giant headquarters building for General Motors in Detroit placed each worker within 20 feet of an operable window. Kahn's factory buildings used extensive glazing and ingenious clerestory systems to bathe factory workers in daylight and to ventilate with little mechanical assistance.

THE FORD MOTOR COMPANY ENGINEERING LABORATORY, designed by Albert Kahn, employs sloping windows to attain more illumination with less glass.

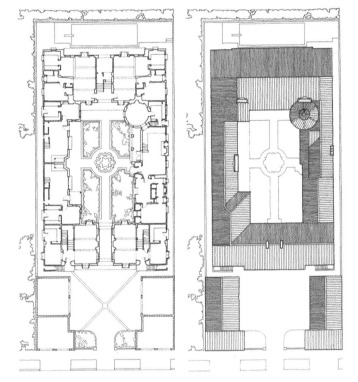

PLAN OF THE ANDALUSIA *West Hollywood, 1926*

COURTYARD HOUSING AT ITS BEST — the Andalusia apartments (1926) in West Hollywood, California, designed by Arthur and Nina Zwebel, who had no formal training in architecture. Buildings with narrow footprints or that wrap around courtyards provide more light and air and use less energy for lighting and illumination. Big, boxy, air-conditioned buildings can be cheaper to build, but we won't be able to afford such power hogs forever.

It's illuminating to compare the footprints of buildings designed before climate control and fluorescent lighting with those built today. Before World War II, large buildings were composed of relatively thin bays and pavilions linked together. With the exception of theaters and auditoriums, every habitable room had a window. More recent buildings have vast areas with no relationship to an outside wall. People occupying these areas are completely isolated from the outside world.

Buildings with narrow footprints—thin buildings whose interior spaces are close to outside walls and windows—consume less energy. Obviously, the closer people are to windows, the less they need electrical illumination. And if those windows can be opened, the building needs less air-conditioning or heat on temperate days.

Buildings with large footprints are power hogs. Vast interior spaces provide little access to windows and rely more on electrical illumination, which generates a lot of heat. So much heat is generated that many of these buildings need year-round air-conditioning. In fact, the era of big boxy buildings came about, not only because they can be cheaper to build, but also because air-conditioning allowed a way to cool them down. These large boxes that require air-conditioning consume even more energy than does a heating system.

In response to this, government agencies now regulate access to windows in buildings; some countries even have regulations requiring sunlight for some rooms. Ironically, some well-intended energy regulations have had the opposite effect, such as those requiring smaller windows that are sealed shut.

This Charter principle proposes solutions for buildings that are more people- and earth-friendly. We can look to examples of this principle at work in pre-war buildings and urban design, and in architectural traditions that vary by culture and climate. In a warm, dry climate, a Mediterranean-style building can be organized around a courtyard humidified by a fountain; the same style building in the hot and humid climate of Florida should be thinner to improve cross-ventilation.

It's important to understand how traditional building types were configured, including how they were placed on the land, how buildings and their rooms were oriented, and the relationship between individual buildings and adjacent ones. Through such an understanding, we can begin to design communities that respect natural systems and people's need for access to them.

"More than any other art form, building and architecture have an interactive relationship with nature. Nature is not only topography and site, but also climate and light.... Built form is necessarily susceptible to an intense interaction with these elements and with time, in its cyclical aspects... yet we tend to forget how universal technology in the form of modern mechanical services (air conditioning, artificial light, etc.) tends towards the elimination of precisely those features that would otherwise relate the outer membrane of a given fabric to a particular place and a specific culture... [and to] natural light in relation to diurnal and seasonal change."

KENNETH FRAMPTON
Center: A Journal for Architecture in America

MARK M. SCHIMMENTI

Mark M. Schimmenti is an architect and urban designer and an associate professor of architecture at the University of Tennessee in Knoxville. In his professional practice, he specializes in creating master plans and comprehensive design guidelines for cities, neighborhoods, and new developments.

Twenty seven

Preservation and renewal of historic buildings, districts, and landscapes affirm the continuity and evolution of urban society.

KEN GREENBERG

Cities are perpetually unfinished serial creations. In each generation, new uses, social patterns, and economic activities emerge, while others become obsolete and are displaced, renewed, or transformed. The form of the city develops through a continuous reworking over the traces of what came before. This nonstop evolution of use and form is both inevitable and desirable.

For this urban evolution to occur successfully, there must be an implied "contract" about the nature of city building in which the contributions of previous generations are understood and creatively reinterpreted, even where change is substantial. In the mid–20th century, however, this contract was broken. The modern movement in city planning and architecture rejected the traditional city as a foundation upon which to build and sought to replace it wholesale. Polemical plans such as Le Corbusier's *Plan Voisin* for Paris (right) proposed the removal of all but a handful of the city's most significant monuments. This approach was widely imitated in urban renewal schemes in North America, most often with disastrous consequences.

This Charter principle affirms New Urbanism's respect for continuity and evolution in the built environment and in landscapes. New Urbanism reinforces the importance of being aware of and honoring the historic fabric of urban places and of designing new urban places that will accommodate change over time. In the United States and

"I believe that when a man
  loses contact with the past
  he loses his soul. Likewise,
  if we deny the architectural
  past—and the lessons to be
  learned from our ancestors
  —then our buildings also
  lose their souls."
CHARLES,
PRINCE OF WALES
A Vision of Britain

"Rest rubble, sprawling
  suburbs, jerry-built,
  Kerwan's mushroom
  house, built of breeze.
  Shelter from the night."
JAMES JOYCE
Ulysses

Canada, this credo is the legacy of the preservation movement that began in the 1960s. When and how this renewed awareness of the importance of the historic urban fabric came about varies from city to city. In Toronto, the nation's centennial celebrations in 1967 inspired a fresh look at the St. Lawrence heritage district, and the city began to focus on the history and architecture of individual buildings and their settings.

Accompanying our renewed commitment to urbanism is a renewed appreciation of both the ability of the traditional city to evolve and the organizational framework of the block, the street, and the building. Defined by the street, the block establishes the underlying context of predictable relationships in which successive generations of buildings and their uses can co-exist harmoniously. By working with, not against, this structure, the whole is not called into question each time the parts change. Though altered in form and meaning, the new is supported by the old.

We are also experiencing a corresponding new regard for historic buildings, districts, and landscapes not just as exceptional artifacts but as living entities, useful sources of precedents, and repositories of enduring urban values. One of the great lessons has been the extraordinary elasticity of urban form. New forms of living, working, recreation, and culture emerge in heritage environments as diverse as Amsterdam's 17th-century canal houses and St. Paul's turn-of-the-century warehouse district. They emerge because, not in spite, of their intrinsic urban qualities—or those qualities of life on the

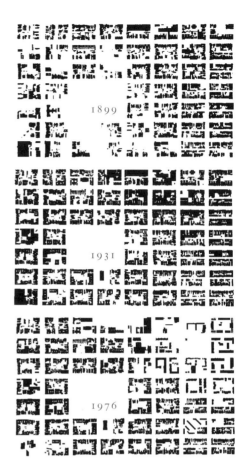

1899

1931

1976

SAN FRANCISCO

street and human relationships that haven't changed all that much, despite alterations in individual buildings and their settings.

In these places and others, such as Charleston, San Francisco (above), Toronto, and New York, the historic fabric continues to evolve and develop new vocations. In each of these cities, there is also an increased understanding of the particular legacy of urban form—block dimensions, street types, and building types. Our understanding of building types and their relationships to the streets of New York, for example, honors the block dimensions of 200 by 800 feet. Evolution is fostered through a combination of techniques, including preservation, adaptive re-use, and strategic new construction.

"The architect should
be regarded as a kind
of physical historian,
because he constructs
relationships across
time: civilization in fact."
VINCENT SCULLY
*American Architecture
and Urbanism*

As the success of these places demonstrates, city form is generally more enduring than particular land uses or functions. The prospects for longevity —continuous preservation and adaptive re-use— are improved where the block, the street, and the building possess a basic generality, simplicity, and adaptability that allow for reasonable degrees of change and modification in response to social, economic, and technological change.

While cities such as Paris and Amsterdam possess a unique and enviable built heritage, the lessons they provide can be generalized. There is no *tabula rasa*. In virtually any setting—existing city or greenfield—there is a significant natural or cultural legacy with landforms, vegetation, watercourses, street patterns, agricultural or industrial heritage, and built forms. The recognition of these elements at any stage of urbanization, as legitimate shapers and influencers of what is to come next, must be an essential part of the methodology of urbanism. Sustained vitality depends upon both stewardship and a skillful layering that builds creatively on the legacies of landscape and urban form.

"In every city there are
individual personalities;
every city possesses a
personal soul formed of
old traditions and living
feelings as well as unre-
solved aspirations. Yet still
the city cannot be inde-
pendent of the general
laws of urban dynamics.
Behind the particular
causes there are general
conditions, and the result
is that no urban growth
is spontaneous. Rather,
it is through the natural
tendencies of the many
groups dispersed through-
out the different parts of
the city that we must
explain the modifications
of the city's structure."
ALDO ROSSI
The Architecture of the City

KEN GREENBERG

Ken Greenberg is an urban designer, architect, and principal of Urban Strategies, a Toronto firm known for its holistic, interdisciplinary approach to city planning and building. Before starting Urban Strategies in 1987, he spent 10 years with the City of Toronto, where he founded and directed the Division of Architecture and Urban Design.

Afterword

In many ways, the Congress for the New Urbanism represents the extension of parallel efforts evolving since Jane Jacobs and William Whyte began their critiques of Modern architecture and the auto-focused metropolis in the 1950s and 1960s. Since that time much work has been undertaken to correct Modernism's negation of the city. It is now generally accepted that a city's vitality is tied to its diversity, human scale, and quality of public space. The notion that the auto-oriented suburb is sustainable or even desirable is no longer conventional wisdom. Environmental groups have developed to defend the ecosystems and farmlands threatened by sprawl. Inner-city activists have mobilized to revitalize urban neighborhoods. Historic preservation groups have expanded their agenda from individual buildings to whole districts and urban economies. The Congress for the New Urbanism builds on all of these movements and attempts to unite them with a common set of principles at three telescoping scales: the region, the neighborhood, and the block.

Like these other contemporary efforts in design and planning, the philosophy of New Urbanism offers an alternative to suburban sprawl, urban decay and disinvestment, single-use zoning, and auto-only environments. Yet it is perhaps unique in developing an interlocking approach at multiple scales. Not since the City Beautiful and Arts-and-Crafts movements at the turn of the century, or the Congres International d'Architecture Moderne (CIAM) in the 1920s, has there been an attempt to create a design vision that unifies the differing scales and disciplines shaping the built environment. Individualized efforts at the scale of the region, the neighborhood, or the street are necessary and important, but not sufficient to bring basic change to our development patterns. The Charter asserts that the three scales are interactive and must be coordinated to have a penetrating effect. This notion that each are interdependent and mutually reinforcing is the result of a new perspective; that the significant increments of our social, economic, and ecological life have shifted from nation, state, and city to globe, region, and neighborhood. We live in a world at once bigger and more immediate than ever before.

The dominance of the global economy, the emergence of metropolitan regions, the maturation of the suburbs, the revitalization of inner-city neighborhoods, and a renewed focus on human-scaled environments are linked contemporary phenomena. Although too often treated independently, each is critically dependent on the other. The global economy's building blocks are regions, not cities or states. Regional policies dramatically affect the evolution of suburbs and the revitalization of the city. Growth and investment in individual neighborhoods indeed depends on regional forces that can reinforce rather than frustrate local initiative. For example, regional initiatives in affordable housing, tax-base sharing, and transportation investments now critically link inner-city neighborhoods to suburban development. Conversely, the physical design of neighborhoods, if allowed to follow the old patterns of sprawl, can easily negate initiatives to preserve open space, reduce traffic congestion, and promote economic equity. And healthy neighborhoods everywhere are dependent on coherent block, street, and building standards as well as supportive regional policies. As the whole is re-conceived, each part changes. This is a precept of the three sections of the Charter.

Too often, New Urbanism is not understood as a complex system of policies and design principles that operate at multiple scales. It is misinterpreted simply as a conservative movement to recapture the past while ignoring the issues of our time. It is thought to be driven by nostalgia and ordered by outdated traditions. To some, New Urbanism simply means tree-lined streets, houses with front porches, and Main Street retail—a reworking of a Norman Rockwell fantasy of small-town America, primarily for the rich.

If such an oversimplification of New Urbanism were true, this criticism would be compelling. But if nostalgic urbanism is such a good idea, why are so many older, traditional neighborhoods in decline? And given the car, the scale of modern business, and the complex nature of families today, is such a nostalgic vision possible or even desirable?

Clearly it is not. But nostalgia is not what New Urbanism is proposing. Its goals and breadth are much grander, more complete and challenging. Many misconceptions are caused by focusing on New Urbanism's neighborhood-scale prescriptions without seeing them embedded in regional structures. Or understanding that those neighborhoods are supported by design principles at the street and building scale that attend more to environmental imperatives and pedestrian comfort than to historical precedent.

Replacing cul-de-sacs and malls with traditional urban design, although desirable, is not sufficient to solve the problems of modern growth, either practically or ideologically. If it were, beautiful historic Main Streets would not be dying across the country, and many urban neighborhoods and first-ring suburbs would not be in decline. If good urban design were enough, then where development happens and who is wealthy enough to afford it would be irrelevant. They are not.

Two tenets of New Urbanism address these critical issues of affordability and location. One is economic diversity. The other is regionalism. Economic diversity calls for a broad range of housing opportunities as well as uses within each neighborhood—affordable and expensive, small and large, rental and ownership, singles and family housing. This is a radical proposition. It implies that more low-income and affordable housing will be built in the wealthy suburbs, while it advocates placing middle-class homes in urban neighborhoods. It advocates mixing income groups and races in a way that frightens many communities. In the city this is labeled "gentrification." In the suburbs, it is called crime (the code word for any housing other than large-lot single family). This principle is rarely realized in practice and, given the current political climate, almost always compromised. But it is a central tenet of New Urbanism and sets a direction quite different from most new development in the suburbs and many urban-renewal programs.

The principle of diversity has a major regional implication: fairly distributed affordable housing for all communities of the region. It implies that we should no longer isolate the poor in the inner city and segregate the middle class in the suburbs. It implies limiting additional public housing in low-income neighborhoods, and instead scattering public housing throughout the region and fostering inclusionary zoning in the suburbs.

Diversity is perhaps the most challenging aspect of New Urbanism, but it is essential to its philosophy. Some have suggested that the consistent and sometimes historical architecture of New Urbanist communities effectively camouflages their underlying economic and social diversity. Certainly the integration of differing housing types and costs

calls for an urban design and architecture that unifies a neighborhood rather than isolates, and in
some cases stigmatizes, its pieces. New Urbanism
may not always succeed in radically reintegrating
the segregated geography of our cities and suburbs,
but it does lay out design and policy principles that
provide the means to do so. The political will to
make such a change consistently involves a larger
cultural challenge.

The aspect of New Urbanism that addresses
the issues of where growth is most appropriate is
its call for regional design. Beyond regional policies
for tax equity or fair-share housing, New Urbanism
proposes to create a definitive physical map of the
metropolis; its boundaries, open spaces, connections,
and centers. This idea of "designing" the region,
much like one could design a neighborhood or
district, has been passé since the time of Daniel
Burnham, the great Chicago planner of the early
20th century. But it is central to addressing the issues
of where development should happen and how it
fits into the whole. Without regional form-givers
like habitat and agricultural preserves, urban growth
boundaries, transit systems, and designated urban
centers, even well-designed neighborhoods can
contribute to sprawl. Infill and redevelopment,
although a high priority for New Urbanism, cannot accommodate all the growth in many regions.
A regional plan is the necessary armature for the
placement of new growth as towns, neighborhoods,
or villages.

Without housing diversity in neighborhoods
and a powerful regional design ordering new
investments, the question of where new development should happen and who can afford it remains
unanswered. Although the challenge of creating
truly diverse neighborhoods and sustainable regional
forms may remain an elusive goal for some time,
the CNU Charter lays out the principles and
techniques to achieve them.

PETER CALTHORPE

Postscript

For five millennia, we built towns and cities with strong centers and clear edges, beyond which lay farms, forests, lakes, and streams. Only in the last five decades have these clear edges become ragged, as the centrifugal forces of sprawl have flung a strange collection of objects across the landscape. The strangest of these objects are big boxes with specialized functions. They are connected to each other by swaths of asphalt. Each is surrounded by a small sea of the same material. Their placement relative to each other and to the smaller boxes we live in is designed and planned for the maximum consumption of time and energy in various forms, including human.

For five millennia, our human settlements were built to human scale, to the five- or ten-minute walk that defined neighborhoods, within which all of life's necessities and many of its frivolities could be found. Even great cities can be seen as a collection of neighborhoods. Greater London is, in fact, a set of towns and villages merged into a metropolis. Even now, Belgravia, Mayfair, Knightsbridge, and Chelsea have distinct centers and edges and distinctive character. Within these neighborhoods, buildings are four or five stories high because that is the maximum number of stairs we could comfortably ascend.

Now we have elevators and cars allowing our cities to expand upward and evermore outward. We have tested the limits of these new toys; emerging economies are pushing these limits even further. It is time for us, however, to recognize that enough is enough. Tall buildings can be exciting in Manhattan and Hong Kong. In cities such as Houston and Atlanta, they merely stunt balanced development by absorbing all the growth potential of a decade onto a handful of sites, leaving parking lots and abandoned buildings a block away. Suburban sprawl, in turn, sucks the economic potential from our cities and saps their ability to renew and regenerate themselves. The result is a blighted environment where once there were working or natural landscapes.

Within cities as well as within natural and working landscapes, complexity and diversity indicate the long-term health, or the sustainability, of these natural and fabricated systems. The earliest ecosystem collapses in our recorded history occurred in the Fertile Crescent, where monoculture farming depleted the fertility on which this early civilization depended. Today's world offers some parallels. Monoculture agriculture seems productive, but it requires alarming quantities of petrochemicals in the form of fertilizers and pesticides, and it depletes soil and pollutes lakes and streams.

In the same way as agriculture, monoculture development patterns had their origin in a good idea: to separate foul steel mills and slaughterhouses from dwellings. Now we rigidly separate all uses— our homes, our workplaces, our children's schools, the places where we assemble. This ensures the maximum consumption of time and energy to move from one place to another. It also separates us from each other. The number of people with whom we have daily contact becomes limited to those we see in our homes and at work. Perhaps we see our neighbors occasionally, but our neighborhoods are not designed to allow us to walk or send our kids to a corner store. They are, frequently, isolated enclaves, behind walls and gates, separating us from anyone whose income or attitudes might differ from ours.

Sustainability means diversity, complexity, and inclusivity. We cannot build sustainable communities based upon monocultural exclusivity. Sustainability also means planning, building, and acting as if tomorrow will in fact come, as if we cared about our grandchildren enough to care about the world we leave them.

The strange objects we have flung about our landscape are built only for today. Most are cheap and shoddy. Grouped into strips (or the American Automobile Slum, as James Howard Kunstler describes such strips), they constitute a hostile and aesthetically offensive environment. And their economic half-life is shrinking. Shopping centers built only in the 1960s are already being abandoned. Their abandonment brings down the values of nearby neighborhoods. WalMarts built five years ago are already being abandoned for superstores.

We have built a world of junk, a degraded environment. It may be profitable for a short term, but its long-term economic prognosis is bleak.

This all began with a compelling vision put forth by General Motors at the 1939 World's Fair. In their Futurama exhibit, the fair's most popular exhibit, GM showed a vision of a utopia, which according to David Gelernter in *1939: The Lost World of the Fair*, was not one of civil society perfected, but a more modest one of middle-class comfort. The key components of Futurama's diorama were a house with a lawn and a ride along uncrowded highways in the privacy and comfort of a private motorcar. These images soon became embedded in our culture's collective consciousness as the new images of the American Dream. After the war, GM's chairman, Charles Wilson, became President Eisenhower's Secretary of Defense. His most memorable public utterance was, "What is good for General Motors is good for the country." The National System of Interstate and Defense Highways program was started during this administration.

Success can seduce us down garden paths that lead to dead ends. The techniques and organizational systems pioneered by Henry Ford helped win World War II. It is not surprising that they were marshaled after the war not just to build cars but also to build houses. The demand for both was fueled by returning soldiers who could spend their savings on cars because their new homes could be financed on easy government terms.

This extraordinary demand for new homes was easier to satisfy by applying mass-production techniques to convert potato fields into Levittowns than by building or renovating houses in older neighborhoods. And mass production meant specialization. So homebuilders churned out these houses, and only houses, in great numbers. Places to shop would be provided in time, but on other sites, by a new group of specialists, who came to be known as shopping-center developers.

After the War, Rosie the Riveter married GI Joe, and she settled down to a life of domesticity. But her new house in Levittown was so isolated from shops, schools, and even neighbors that a second car became a necessity. In time, her house had to grow, to accommodate the stuff that prosperity and consumerism demanded. Her daughters, whose expectations of material comfort were yet higher, later found it necessary to commute to work, to escape the isolation and emptiness of suburban life, as well as to support a consumer culture developed to fill the emptiness of suburban life.

City life no longer provided an alternative since the flight to the suburbs had stripped cities, which found it increasingly difficult to provide such basic services as safe streets and good schools. Attractive and convenient public transportation was even more difficult to provide. By the time the Interstate system was under way, GM (and others) had bought up and dismantled many of our cities' trolley systems. Without this alternative way of getting around, and with most of us scattered too far apart for any form of public transit to work, we became two- and three-car families, a vision even Futurama had not dared to predict.

The utopia of comfort turned out to be flawed. By now the dream has become a nightmare for many. The average Sunbelt family makes at least 14 car trips per day and spends more than $14,000 a year on two cars (as well as spending, cumulatively, about six weeks each year encapsulated in them, often stuck in traffic). We kill nearly as many people per year in traffic accidents (about 44,000) as were killed in Vietnam. We spend $50 billion annually to maintain a military presence in the Persian Gulf to protect our dependence on foreign oil.

It doesn't have to be this way. Through the 1920s, well into the automobile age, we built mixed-use, pedestrian-scale communities with strong centers and clear edges. In most cities, these 1920s neighborhoods (among them Kansas City's Country Club District, Lake Forest near Chicago, Atlanta's Inman Park, and Mountain Brook in Birmingham, Alabama) are still the most desirable places to live. They cope gracefully with cars because they are designed for people at a human scale. They represent the culmination of centuries of post-Renaissance thinking about the Ideal City, which centers around the scale of the Vitruvian man whose outstretched arms and legs describe a circle,

that most perfect of geometric forms. This in turn symbolized the clear edge of the Ideal City, within which, sheltered by community, we can live in harmony with the natural world, but with respect for the awesome and sometimes awful power of Mother Nature.

The New Urbanism is no more than an attempt to pick up the threads, so recently abandoned, of this 5,000-year-old craft of building towns and cities. For most of the past 500 years, since Alberti and Serlio rediscovered Vitruvius and the wisdom of the ancients, this craft has been refined by succeeding generations. We have only recently turned away from our obligation to carry on the traditions of this craft and to add to this body of knowledge. Instead we engaged in a radical experiment to create a "Brave New World," a Futurama.

The 50-year-old experiment has failed miserably. Once a magical machine for mobility, the automobile has been turned into an indispensable appliance and a prison that separates us from contact with our fellow citizens. Our countryside is devastated and our cities partly abandoned. But we can rebuild our cities and towns. We can stop the despoiling of our countryside. We can work together as environmentalists and advocates for social justice, as architects and planners, as developers of humane settlements, and as long-term investors in our land.

ROBERT DAVIS

Robert Davis is the Chair of the Congress for the New Urbanism and the founder of Seaside, Florida. He is a principal in Arcadia Land Company, a San Francisco firm specializing in town building and land stewardship.

Editors' Notes

We live in the kind of traditional neighborhood our parents took for granted (and later happily rejected for the suburbs). Many of our mornings begin walking our two kids to their neighborhood schools. A block away, we can catch a bus downtown, and if we have business in Denver, a transfer to an inter-city bus brings us there quickly. We walk or bike to the library and to do errands at our neighborhood shopping center. On summer nights, we stroll to a neighborhood park where people enjoy a large playground, volleyball, picnics, and sunsets.

Ours is the type of convenient, sane, and compact neighborhood that is now becoming rare and exclusive. What was once taken for granted—handy services, mixed uses, good schools, safe streets, efficient transit—has become exotic, or is regarded as "amenity" that causes homebuyers to enter bidding wars over 1950 brick boxes.

We became involved in the New Urbanism (and, before that, historic preservation) because we believe in preserving and enhancing the best elements in neighborhoods like ours. We would also like to see other compact communities flourish as a benefit to our nation's economic, environmental, and, yes, mental health.

The authors who contributed to this effort are all too aware of the superannuated zoning, banking, policy, and real-estate practices that discourage good planning and development. In many cases they are the leaders who sounded the national alarm about the consequences of poorly shaped growth. But they are also visionaries with solutions based on a hopeful message. Desperate city neighborhoods can be renewed; atomized suburbs can be patched together; and traditional communities, natural areas, and farmlands can still be saved.

We are grateful for the guidance of the CNU Board; especially for the contributions of an advisory committee that included Jonathan Barnett, Peter Calthorpe, and Daniel Solomon. They championed the book and spent hours consulting on its graphic look and content. We are thankful for the cooperation of all 32 authors, who volunteered to write the essays and withstood our hounding during revisions. We genuflect to Shelley Poticha, an exemplar of level-headedness and clear-eyed criticism. Her confidence and enthusiasm never wavered. Terri Wolfe provided expert editorial as well as graphic guidance. Will Fleissig introduced us to CNU and provided advice and support. CNU staffers, especially Andy Shafer, offered invaluable assistance and research. We also thank our families for their support, especially David and Joanne McCormick, Angela McCormick, Gaetana Leccese, Alice Leccese Powers, and Maria Leccese Kotch. Our children Nora and Vito— budding New Urbanists—entertained each other while this project washed over several rooms of our home. Pedestrian extraordinaire, Dan DiSanto of Brooklyn, New York, taught one of the editors at an early age how to explore the city by foot and train.

We hope this book makes a difference.

MICHAEL LECCESE AND KATHLEEN McCORMICK

Michael Leccese and Kathleen McCormick are co-principals of Fountainhead Communications, Inc., in Boulder, Colorado. They have written and edited numerous books and write for publications including *Architecture*, *Landscape Architecture*, *Metropolis*, *The New York Times*, *Preservation*, *Planning*, and *Urban Land*.

Credits

COVER

Left: New Jersey regional map illustration from *A Region at Risk*, courtesy of the Regional Plan Association's "Visual Simulations for the Region's Future." This program was developed as part of the Regional Design Program led by Robert D. Yaro with Jonathan Barnett, Harry L. Dodson and Dodson Associates, and Robert L. Geddes. Center: Communications Hill, San Jose, California. Designed by Solomon Architecture and Urban Design. Illustration courtesy of Daniel Solomon. Right: Haymount, Caroline County, Virginia. Designed by Duany Plater-Zyberk & Company. Illustration courtesy of Andres Duany and Elizabeth Plater-Zyberk, Duany Plater-Zyberk & Company.

PAGE 4

Downtown Boston. Photograph provided by Local Government Commission.

PAGE 11

Downtown Athens, Georgia. Photograph provided by Shelley Poticha, Congress for the New Urbanism.

PAGE 12

New Jersey regional map illustration, from *A Region at Risk*. Courtesy of the Regional Plan Association.

PAGE 17

Envision Utah Alternative Growth Strategies, Salt Lake City, Utah. Designed by Calthorpe Associates. Illustration courtesy of Peter Calthorpe.

PAGE 18

The Land Use, Transportation, and Air Quality Connection (LUTRAQ) plan for Washington County, Oregon. Designed by Calthorpe Associates. Illustration courtesy of Calthorpe Associates and 1000 Friends of Oregon.

PAGE 20

Photographs by Alex MacLean, Landslides.

PAGE 21

Photograph by Lynn Johnson.

PAGE 22

Top and bottom left: New Jersey regional map illustrations from *A Region at Risk*. Courtesy of the Regional Plan Association. Right: Diagram provided by Robert D. Yaro.

PAGE 25

Diagrams courtesy of Robert D. Yaro.

PAGE 26

Illustrations courtesy of Robert D. Yaro and Dodson Associates.

PAGE 28

Photograph by Alex MacLean, Landslides.

PAGES 30 & 31

Illustration from *Rural by Design*. Courtesy of Randall Arendt, Natural Lands Trust.

PAGE 33

Photographs by Alex MacLean, Landslides.

PAGE 34

Photograph courtesy of Randall Arendt.

PAGES 36, 37 & 38

Community Initiative plan for West Garfield Park, Chicago. Designed by Farr Associates. Illustrations courtesy of Douglas Farr.

PAGE 39

Photograph courtesy of Shelley Poticha.

PAGE 40

Oakland Arts District. Simulation by Steve Price, Urban Advantage.

PAGE 42

Jindalee Town, Perth, Australia, designed by Ecologically Sustainable Design. Illustration courtesy of Wendy Morris, Ecologically Sustainable Design.

PAGE 44

Garden-City diagram from *Garden Cities of To-morrow* by Ebenezer Howard.

PAGE 45

Photograph courtesy of Doug Shoemaker, Mission Housing.

PAGES 46 & 47

Eastgate Mall, Chattanooga, Tennessee. Designed by Dover, Kohl & Partners. Illustrations courtesy of Joseph Kohl, Dover, Kohl & Partners.

PAGE 48

Photograph of Annapolis, Maryland, by Alex MacLean, Landslides.

PAGE 50

Top: Indianapolis, Indiana. Bottom: Cleveland, Ohio. Photographs by Alex MacLean, Landslides.

PAGE 51

Illustration by Christopher Alexander from *The Timeless Way of Building*.

PAGE 52

Vermont Village Plaza, South Central Los Angeles, designed by Solomon Architecture and Urban Design. Photographs and illustration courtesy of Solomon Architecture and Urban Design. Photographs by Grant Mudford.

PAGE 55

Top left: Vest Pocket
Community, Fairfax,
California, designed by
Solomon Architecture
and Urban Design.
Photograph courtesy of
Solomon Architecture
and Urban Design. Photo-
graph by Bambi LaPlante.
Top right: Photograph
courtesy of Douglas
Kelbaugh. Lower right and
bottom: Photographs cour-
tesy of Local Government
Commission.

PAGE 59

Photograph courtesy of
G. B. Arrington, Tri-Met,
Portland, Oregon.

PAGE 60

Top: Region 2040 plan.
Courtesy of Metro,
Portland, Oregon.
Bottom: Gresham Central
on Portland, Oregon's MAX
light-rail line. Photograph
by Steven Bealf.

PAGE 61

Civic Stadium Joint
Development project,
Portland, Oregon.
Photograph by
Steven Bealf.

PAGE 62

The Round, Beaverton,
Oregon, designed by
StastnyBrun Architects.
Illustration and photograph
courtesy of G. B. Arrington.
Photograph by
Steven Bealf.

PAGE 63

Top: Photograph provided
by G. B. Arrington.
Bottom: Photograph
courtesy of Local
Government Commission.

PAGE 64

Photograph by
Tony Stone Images.

PAGE 66

Minneapolis region
property value map
courtesy of Myron Orfield,
State Representative of
Minnesota.

PAGE 68

Diagram center photogra-
phy by Local Government
Commission. Diagram
outer photography by
Alex MacLean, Landslides.

PAGE 70

Communications Hill,
San Jose, California,
designed by Solomon
Architecture and Urban
Design. Illustration courtesy
of Solomon Architecture
and Urban Design.

PAGE 75

Mizner Park, Boca Raton,
Florida, designed by
Cooper Carry, Inc.
Photographs courtesy of
Cooper Carry, Inc.

PAGE 76

Left: Urban neighborhood
diagram provided by Duany
Plater-Zyberk & Company.
Right: Rural neighborhood
diagram by Clarence Perry,
courtesy of Jonathan
Barnett, University of
Pennsylvania.

PAGE 77

Transit-oriented develop-
ment diagram courtesy of
Calthorpe Associates.

PAGES 78 & 79

Illustrations by Leon Krier.

PAGE 80

Illustration by Clarence
Stein and Henry Wright.
Courtesy of Duany Plater-
Zyberk & Company.

PAGE 81

Photograph provided by
Duany Plater-Zyberk &
Company.

PAGE 82

West Sacramento neighbor-
hood center, Sacramento,
California. Designed by
Duany Plater-Zyberk &
Company. Illustration
courtesy of Duany Plater-
Zyberk & Company.

PAGE 84

Top and bottom: Photo-
graphs by Alex MacLean,
Landslides. Center:
Conventional trip assign-
ment vs. traditional trip
assignment diagram.
Courtesy of Walter Kulash,
Glatting Jackson Kercher
Anglin Lopez Rinehart.

PAGE 86

Photograph by Peter Katz,
Urban Advantage.

PAGE 87

Cathedral City, California.
Designed by Freedman,
Tung & Bottomley.
Illustration courtesy
of Freedman, Tung &
Bottomley.

PAGES 88 & 89

Pleasant View Gardens,
Baltimore, a HOPE VI
project. Designed by Torti
Gallas and Partners/CHK,
Inc. Photographs and
illustrations courtesy of
John Torti, Torti Gallas
and Partners/CHK, Inc.

PAGE 90

The Townhomes on Capitol
Hill, Washington, D.C., a
HOPE VI project.
Designed by Weinstein
Associates.
Top left and right:
Photographs by Shelley
Poticha. Center and
bottom: Photographs
and illustrations courtesy
of Amy Weinstein,
Weinstein Associates.

PAGE 91

Randolph neighborhood
revitalization, Richmond,
Virginia. Designed by
Urban Design Associates.
Photographs courtesy
of Ray Gindroz, Urban
Design Associates.

PAGE 92

Crawford Square,
Pittsburgh, Pennsylvania.
Designed by Urban Design
Associates. Photographs
courtesy of Urban Design
Associates.

PAGE 94

Diggs Town, Norfolk,
Virginia. Designed by
Urban Design Associates.
Photographs courtesy
of Urban Design Associates.

PAGE 95
Horner Homes, Chicago, Illinois, a HOPE VI project. Designed by Calthorpe Associates. Illustrations and photographs courtesy of Calthorpe Associates.

PAGES 96 & 98
Photographs courtesy of John Norquist, Mayor of Milwaukee.

PAGE 99
Transit Mall, San Jose, California. Photograph by Michael Corbett.

PAGE 100
Photograph of downtown Portland, Oregon, courtesy of G. B. Arrington.

PAGE 101
Photograph courtesy of William Lieberman, San Diego Metropolitan Transit District.

PAGE 102
Photographs courtesy of Calthorpe Associates.

PAGE 103
Diagram courtesy of New Jersey Transit, from *Planning for Transit-Friendly Land Use: A Handbook for New Jersey Communities.*

PAGE 104
Civano Neighborhood, Tucson, Arizona. Designed by Moule & Polyzoides Architects and Urbanists. Illustrations courtesy of Elizabeth Moule, Moule & Polyzoides Architects and Urbanists.

PAGE 105
Top: Photograph courtesy of Moule & Polyzoides Architects and Urbanists. Bottom: Photograph by Alex MacLean, Landslides.

PAGE 106
Photograph and illustration courtesy of Dan Burden, Walkable Communities, Inc.

PAGE 107
Rachel Carson Elementary School at Kentlands, Gaithersburg, Maryland. Designed by Duany Plater-Zyberk & Company. Photograph provided by Peter Katz, Urban Advantage.

PAGE 108
Colonial Williamsburg code. Illustration courtesy of Bill Lennertz, Lennertz Coyle & Associates.

PAGE 110
Kentlands photograph courtesy of Duany Plater-Zyberk & Company. Wilsonville, Oregon code, designed by Lennertz Coyle & Associates. Illustration courtesy of Bill Lennertz, Lennertz Coyle & Associates.

PAGE 111
Redmond, Oregon, neighborhood plan. Designed by Lennertz Coyle & Associates. Illustration courtesy of Bill Lennertz.

PAGE 113
Photograph courtesy of Tom Comitta, Thomas Comitta Associates, Inc.

PAGES 114 & 115
Milwaukee RiverWalk, Milwaukee, Wisconsin. Designed by Ken Kay Associates. Illustrations and photographs provided by Ken Kay.

PAGE 116
Left: Photograph courtesy of Calthorpe Associates. Center: Photograph courtesy of Tom Comitta. Right: Mizner Park, Boca Raton, Florida. Photograph courtesy of Cooper Carry, Inc.

PAGE 117
Top left: Photograph courtesy of Doug Shoemaker. Top right: Photograph courtesy of Peter Katz. Bottom: Kimberly Park, Winston-Salem, North Carolina, a HOPE VI project. Designed by Urban Design Associates. Illustration courtesy of Urban Design Associates.

PAGE 118
The Crossings, Mountain View, California, designed by Calthorpe Associates. Illustrations and photographs courtesy of Calthorpe Associates.

PAGE 120
Haymount, Caroline County, Virginia. Designed by Duany Plater-Zyberk & Company. Illustration courtesy of Duany Plater-Zyberk & Company.

PAGE 123
Photograph courtesy of Daniel Solomon.

PAGE 124
Left: South Park, San Francisco, California. Aerial photograph courtesy of the City of San Francisco. South Park photographs courtesy of Christopher J. Hudson, Congress for the New Urbanism.

PAGE 125
Illustration courtesy of Colin Rowe and Fred Koetter.

PAGE 126
101 San Fernando, San Jose, California. Designed by Solomon Architecture and Urban Design. Illustration courtesy of Solomon Architecture and Urban Design.

PAGE 128
Photographs courtesy of Moule & Polyzoides Architects and Urbanists.

PAGE 129
University of Arizona, Tucson. Designed by Moule & Polyzoides Architects and Urbanists. Photographs and drawings courtesy of Moule & Polyzoides Architects and Urbanists.

PAGE 131
Windsor, Florida.
Urban design by Duany
Plater-Zyberk & Company.
Top: Windsor Tennis Club.
Architecture by Jorge
Hernandez, Dennis Hector,
and Joanna Lombard.
Photograph by Thomas
Delbeck. Center: Photo-
graph by Thomas Delbeck.
Bottom left: Architecture by
Gibson and Slickworth.
Photograph by Thomas
Delbeck. Bottom middle:
Architecture by Scott
Merrill. Photograph by
Xavier Iglesias. Bottom
right: Architecture by Hugh
Newell Jacobsen. Photo-
graph by Thomas Delbeck.
Photographs courtesy of
Duany Plater-Zyberk &
Company.

PAGE 132
Kelbaugh residence,
Princeton, New Jersey.
Designed by Douglas
Kelbaugh. Photograph and
illustration courtesy of
Douglas Kelbaugh.

PAGE 133
Randolph Neighborhood,
Richmond, Virginia.
Designed by Urban Design
Associates. Photograph
courtesy of Urban Design
Associates.

PAGE 134
Top: Celebration, Florida.
Urban design by Cooper,
Robertson & Partners.
Pattern Book by Urban
Design Associates.
Bottom left: Randolph
Neighborhood, Richmond,
Virginia. Designed by
Urban Design Associates.
Bottom right: Diggs Town,
Norfolk, Virginia. Photo-
graph by Paul Rocheleau.
All photographs courtesy of
Urban Design Associates.

PAGE 135
Top: Photograph courtesy
of Urban Design Associates.
Bottom: Photograph
courtesy of Calthorpe
Associates.

PAGE 136
Top: College Homes, a
HOPE VI project in
Knoxville, Tennessee.
Designed by Urban Design
Associates. Illustration
courtesy of Urban Design
Associates. Bottom: Forest
Park Southeast Revitalization
Plan, St. Louis. Before and
after illustrations courtesy of
Urban Design Associates.

PAGE 137
College Homes, a HOPE VI
project in Knoxville,
Tennessee. Before and after
illustrations courtesy of
Urban Design Associates.

PAGE 138
Bryant Park, New York City.
Photograph and plan
courtesy of Grand Central
Partnership/Bryant Park
Restoration Corporation.
Photograph by F. Charles.

PAGE 139
Bryant Park, New York City.
Photograph courtesy of
Gianni Longo, American
Communities Partnership.
Inset image of graffiti
provided by Tony Stone
Images.

PAGE 140
Mizner Park, Boca Raton,
Florida. Photograph
courtesy of Cooper
Carry, Inc.

PAGE 142
Top left: Mountain View,
California. Designed by
Freedman Tung &
Bottomley. Photograph
courtesy of Freedman
Tung & Bottomley.
Top right: Photograph
courtesy of Local
Government Commission.
Bottom: Photograph by
Dan Burden.

PAGE 143
Redmond Town Center,
Redmond, Washington.
Designed by LMN
Architects. Illustration and
photographs courtesy
of LMN Architects.

PAGE 144
Top: Photograph courtesy
of Shelley Poticha. Bottom
left: Photograph courtesy
of Moule & Polyzoides
Architects and Urbanists.
Bottom right: Photograph
by Judy Corbett, Local
Government Commission.

PAGE 145
State Street, Chicago.
Photograph by Shelley
Poticha.

PAGE 146
Street design simulation
by Steve Price, Urban
Advantage.

PAGE 148
Left: Photograph courtesy
of Victor Dover, Dover,
Kohl & Partners.
Right: Photograph
courtesy of Peter Katz.

PAGE 149
Illustrations courtesy of
Victor Dover, Dover,
Kohl & Partners.

PAGE 150
Top left: Photograph
courtesy of Peter Katz.
Top right and bottom:
Photograph and illustration
courtesy of Dover, Kohl
& Partners.

PAGE 151
West Palm Beach, Florida.
Master plan designed by
Duany Plater-Zyberk &
Company. Illustrations and
photographs courtesy of
Duany Plater-Zyberk &
Company. Photograph top
right by L. Fontalvo-Abello.

PAGE 153
Top: Laguna West,
Sacramento County,
California. Designed by
Calthorpe Associates.
Photograph courtesy
of Calthorpe Associates.
Center: Photograph courtesy
of Local Government
Commission.
Bottom: Post Office Square,
Boston, Massachusetts.
Photograph courtesy of
Gianni Longo.

PAGE 154
Roosevelt Solar Village,
Roosevelt, New Jersey.
Designed by Kelbaugh+
Lee. Photographs and
illustrations courtesy
of Douglas Kelbaugh.

PAGE 156
Photograph courtesy
of Shelley Poticha.

PAGE 157
Top: Photograph by
Douglas Kelbaugh.
Bottom: Photograph by
Alex MacLean, Landslides.

PAGE 158
The Pedestrian Pocket
model designed by
Calthorpe Associates.
Illustration courtesy of
Calthorpe Associates.

PAGE 160
Photograph courtesy
of Duany Plater-Zyberk
& Company.

PAGE 161
Illustrations by Leon Krier.

PAGE 162
Photograph courtesy of
Duany Plater-Zyberk &
Company.

PAGE 163
Top: Temple for Seaside,
Seaside, Florida, designed
by Roberto M. Behar.
Illustration courtesy of
Duany Plater-Zyberk &
Company. Far right:
Photograph courtesy of
John Norquist. Bottom:
Photograph courtesy of
Shelley Poticha.

PAGE 164
Top: Doolittle Map of
New Haven, 1824. Bottom:
Diagram of town squares
from The Lexicon of the New
Urbanism. Courtesy of
Duany Plater-Zyberk &
Company.

PAGE 165
Seaside, Florida. Diagrams
courtesy of Duany Plater-
Zyberk & Company.

PAGE 167
Illustration by Leon Krier.

PAGES 168 & 169
Photographs and illustrations
courtesy of The Albert
Kahn Collaborative, Inc.

PAGE 170
Photographs by Julius
Shulman. Photographs and
illustrations courtesy of
Moule & Polyzoides
Architects and Urbanists.

PAGE 172
Photograph by
Alex MacLean, Landslides.

PAGE 173
Le Corbusier's Plan Voisin
for Paris. Courtesy of
Michael Dennis.

PAGE 174
Left: Denver Dry Goods
renovation, Denver,
Colorado. Photographs
courtesy of Jonathan Rose,
Affordable Housing
Development Corporation.
Right: Alamo Square,
San Francisco. Illustration
courtesy of Anne Vernez
Moudon.

PAGE 175
Photograph courtesy
of Duany Plater-Zyberk
& Company.

ALEXANDER, CHRISTOPHER. *A Pattern Language: Towns, Buildings, Construction*. New York University Press, 1977.

ALEXANDER, CHRISTOPHER. *The Timeless Way of Building*. New York University Press, 1977.

ARENDT, RANDALL et al. *Rural by Design: Maintaining Small Town Character*. APA Planners Press, 1994.

BACHELARD, GASTON. *The Poetics of Space*. Beacon Press, 1994.

BACON, EDMUND N. *Design of Cities*. Penguin Books, 1974.

BALDASSARE, MARK. *Trouble in Paradise: The Suburban Transformation in America*. Columbia University Press, 1988.

BARNETT, JONATHAN. *The Elusive City: Five Centuries of Design, Ambition and Miscalculation*. Harper & Row, 1986.

BARNETT, JONATHAN. *The Fractured Metropolis: Improving the New City, Restoring the Old City, Reshaping the Region*. HarperCollins, 1995.

BEL GEDDES, NORMAN. *Magic Motorways*. Random House, 1940.

BERRY, JEFFREY et al. *The Rebirth of Urban Democracy*. Brookings Institution, 1993.

BEVERIDGE, CHARLES E. et al. *Frederick Law Olmsted: Designing the American Landscape*. Rizzoli, 1995.

BLAKE, PETER. *Form Follows Fiasco*. Little, Brown, 1974.

BOLLIER, DAVID. *How Smart Growth Can Stop Sprawl: A Fledgling Citizen Movement Expands*. Essential Books, 1998.

BRAND, STEWART. *How Buildings Learn: What Happens After They're Built*. Viking, 1994.

BREEN, ANN AND DICK RIGBY. *Waterfronts: Cities Reclaim Their Edge*. McGraw-Hill, 1994.

BROOKE, STEVEN. *Seaside*. Pelican, 1995.

BUDER, STANLEY. *Visionaries and Planners: The Garden City Movement and the Modern Community*. Oxford University Press, 1990.

BURNHAM, DANIEL. *Plan of Chicago*. Princeton Architectural Press, 1994.

CALTHORPE, PETER. *The Next American Metropolis: Ecology, Community, and the American Dream*. Princeton Architectural Press, 1993.

CHARLES, PRINCE OF WALES. *A Vision of Britain: A Personal View of Architecture*. Doubleday, 1989.

CISNEROS, HENRY (ed.). *Interwoven Destinies: Cities and the Nation*. W.W. Norton, 1993.

DENNIS, MICHAEL. *Court and Garden: from the French hotel to the city of modern architecture*. MIT Press, 1986.

DOWNS, ANTHONY. *New Visions for Metropolitan America*. Brookings Institution/Lincoln Institute of Land Policy, 1994.

DOWNS, ANTHONY. *Stuck In Traffic: Coping With Peak-Hour Traffic Congestion*. Brookings Institution, 1992.

DUANY, ANDRES. *The Lexicon of the New Urbanism*. Duany Plater-Zyberk & Company, 1999.

DUANY, ANDRES AND ELIZABETH PLATER-ZYBERK. *Towns and Townmaking Principles*. Rizzoli, 1991.

EASTERLING, KELLER. *American Town Plans: A Comparative Time Line*. Princeton Architectural Press, 1993.

ECKBO, GARRETT. *Urban Landscape Design*. McGraw-Hill, 1964.

ETZIONI, AMITAI. *The Spirit of Community: The Reinvention of American Society*. Simon & Schuster, 1994.

FISHMAN, ROBERT. *Bourgeois Utopias: The Rise and Fall of Suburbia*. Basic Books, 1989.

FITCH, JAMES MARSTON. *Historic Preservation: Curatorial Management of the Built World*. University of Virginia Press, 1990.

Bibliography

FRAMPTON, KENNETH. "Ten Points for an Architecture of Regionalism: A Provisional Polemic." *Center: A Journal of Architecture in America*, Vol. 3, 1987.

GALLAGHER, WINIFRED. *The Power of Place: How Our Surroundings Shape Our Thoughts, Emotions, and Actions*. Poseidon Press, 1993.

GARREAU, JOEL. *Edge City: Life on the New Frontier*. Doubleday, 1991.

GARVIN, ALEXANDER. *The American City: What Works, What Doesn't*. McGraw-Hill, 1996.

GEHL, JAN. *Life Between Buildings — Using Public Space*. Van Nostrand Reinhold, 1987.

GODDARD, STEPHEN B. *Getting There: The Epic Struggle between Road and Rail in the Twentieth Century*. University of Chicago Press, 1994.

GRATZ, ROBERTA BRANDES AND NORMAN MINTZ. *Cities Back From the Edge: New Life For Downtown*. John Wiley and Sons, 1998.

HALE, JONATHAN. *The Old Way of Seeing: How Architecture Lost Its Magic (And How to Get It Back)*. Houghton Mifflin, 1994.

HEGEMANN, WERNER AND ELBERT PEETS. *American Vitruvius: An Architect's Handbook of Civic Art*. Princeton Architectural Press, 1988.

HILDEBRAND, GRANT. *Designing for Industry: The Architecture of Albert Kahn*. MIT Press, 1974.

HISS, TONY. *The Experience of Place*. Vintage Books, 1991.

HOWARD, EBENEZER. *Garden Cities of To-morrow*. Faber and Faber, 1945.

HYLTON, THOMAS. *Save Our Land, Save Our Towns: A Plan for Pennsylvania*. RB Books, 1995.

JACKSON, FRANK. *Sir Raymond Unwin: Architect, Planner, and Visionary*. Zwemmer Books, 1987.

JACKSON, KENNETH T. *Crabgrass Frontier: The Suburbanization of the United States*. Oxford University Press, 1987.

JACOBS, ALLAN B. *Great Streets*. MIT Press, 1993.

JACOBS, ALLAN B. *Looking at Cities*. Harvard University Press, 1985.

JACOBS, JANE. *Cities and the Wealth of Nations: Principles of Economic Life*. Random House, 1985.

JACOBS, JANE. *The Death and Life of Great American Cities*. Vintage Books, 1992.

KAHN, LOUIS I. *Between Silence and Light*. Random House, 1979.

KATZ, PETER. *The New Urbanism: Toward an Architecture of Community*. McGraw-Hill, 1994.

KAY, JANE HOLTZ. *Asphalt Nation: How the Automobile Took Over America, and How We Can Take It Back*. Crown Publishers, 1997.

KELBAUGH, DOUGLAS. *Common Place: Toward Neighborhood and Regional Design*. University of Washington Press, 1997.

KELBAUGH, DOUGLAS (ed.). *The Pedestrian Pocket Book: A New Suburban Design Strategy*. Princeton Architectural Press, 1989.

KEMMIS, DANIEL. *Community and the Politics of Place*. University of Oklahoma Press, 1990.

KEMMIS, DANIEL. *The Good City and The Good Life: Renewing the Sense of Community*. Houghton Mifflin, 1995.

KOSTOF, SPIRO. *The City Assembled: The Elements of Urban Form through History*. Bulfinch Press, 1992.

KOSTOF, SPIRO. *The City Shaped: Urban Patterns and Meanings through History*. Bulfinch Press, 1994.

KRIER, LEON. *Architecture and Urban Design, 1967–1992*. St. Martin's Press, 1992.

KRIER, ROB. *Urban Space*. Rizzoli, 1979.

KUNSTLER, JAMES HOWARD. *Home from Nowhere: Remaking our Everyday World for the 21st Century*. Simon & Schuster, 1996.

KUNSTLER, JAMES HOWARD. *The Geography of Nowhere: The Rise and Decline of America's Man-Made Landscape*. Simon & Schuster, 1994.

LANGDON, PHILIP. *A Better Place To Live: Reshaping the American Suburb*. Harper Perennial, 1995.

LEGATES, RICHARD T. AND FREDERIC STOUT (eds.). *The City Reader*. Routeledge, 1996.

LEJEUNE, JEAN-FRANCOIS (ed.). *The New City*. Vol. 1–3. University of Miami School of Architecture/ Princeton Architectural Press, 1994.

LONGO, GIANNI. *A Guide to Great American Public Places*. Urban Initiatives, 1996.

LYNCH, KEVIN. *The Image of the City*. MIT Press, 1960.

MACKAYE, BENTON. *The New Exploration: A Philosophy of Regional Planning*. University of Illinois Press, 1994.

MADDEX, DIANE (ed.). *All About Old Buildings: The Whole Preservation Catalog*. The Preservation Press, 1985.

MCCAMANT, KATHRYN AND CHARLES DURRETT. *CoHousing, A Contemporary Approach to Housing Ourselves*. Ten Speed Press, 1994.

MCHARG, IAN. *Design With Nature*. Wiley, 1995.

MOE, RICHARD AND CARTER WILKIE. *Changing Places: Rebuilding Community in the Age of Sprawl*. Henry Holt, 1997.

MOHNEY, DAVID. *Seaside: Making a Town in America*. Princeton Architectural Press, 1991.

MORRISH, WILLIAM. *Planning to Stay*. Milkweed Press, 1994.

MOUDON, ANNE VERNEZ. *Built for Change: Neighborhood Architecture in San Francisco*. MIT Press, 1986.

MUMFORD, LEWIS. *The City in History: Its Origins, Its Transformations, and Its Prospects*. Harcourt, Brace & World, 1961.

MUMFORD, LEWIS. *The Highway and the City*. Harcourt, Brace & World, 1964.

NELESSON, ANTON. *Visions for a New American Dream: Process, Principles, and an Ordinance to Plan and Design Small Communities*. APA Planners Press, 1993.

NORBERG-SCHULZ, CHRISTIAN. *Genius Loci: Towards a Phenomenology of Architecture*. Rizzoli, 1980.

NORQUIST, JOHN. *The Wealth of Cities: Revitalizing the Centers of American Life*. Addison Wesley, 1998.

OLDENBURG, RAY. *The Great Good Place*. Paragon House, 1991.

ORFIELD, MYRON. *Metropolitics: A Regional Agenda for Community and Stability*. Brookings Institution/Lincoln Institute of Land Policy, 1997.

PICK, MARITZA. *The Sierra Club Guide to Community Organizing: How to Save Your Neighborhood, City, or Town*. Sierra Club Books, 1993.

POLYZOIDES, STEFANOS et al. *Courtyard Housing in Los Angeles: A Typological Analysis*. Princeton Architectural Press, 1992.

PORTER, DOUGLAS R. *Managing Growth in America's Communities*. Island Press, 1997.

REICH, ROBERT B. *The Work of Nations: Preparing Ourselves for 21st Century Capitalism*. Random House, 1992.

REPS, JOHN. *The Making of Urban America: A History of City Planning in the U.S.* Princeton University Press, 1965, 1994.

ROSSI, ALDO. *The Architecture of the City*. MIT Press, 1982.

ROWE, COLIN AND FRED KOETTER. *Collage City*. MIT Press, 1978.

RUDOFSKY, BERNARD. *Streets for People*. Van Nostrand Reinhold, 1969.

RUSK, DAVID. *Cities Without Suburbs*. Woodrow Wilson Center Press, 1995.

RYBCZYNSKI, WITOLD. *City Life*. Scribner, 1995.

SCULLY, VINCENT. *American Architecture and Urbanism*. Henry Holt, 1969.

SCULLY, VINCENT. *Architecture: The Natural and the Manmade*. St. Martins Press, 1993.

SENNETT, RICHARD. *The Conscience of the Eye: The Design and Social Life of Cities*. W. W. Norton, 1992.

SENNETT, RICHARD. *The Fall of Public Man*. W. W. Norton, 1992.

SEWELL, JOHN. *The Shape of the City: Toronto Struggles With Modern Planning*. University of Toronto Press, 1993.

SMITH, WENDY. "The Ideal City: Raising children successfully in a city is not only possible, it can be good for them—not to mention their parents." *Preservation*, November/December 1998.

SOLOMON, DANIEL. *Rebuilding*. Princeton Architectural Press, 1992.

SORKIN, MICHAEL (ed.). *Variations on a Theme Park: The New American City and the End of Public Space*. The Noonday Press, 1992.

SPIRN, ANNE WHISTON. *The Granite Garden: Urban Nature and Human Design*. Basic Books, 1984.

SUCHER, DAVID. *City Comforts*. City Comforts Press, 1995.

THOMPSON, J. WILLIAM. "LA Forum: Is There a Prescription for Sprawl?" *Landscape Architecture*, September 1998.

UNWIN, RAYMOND. *Town Planning in Practice: An Introduction to the Art of Designing Cities and Suburbs*. 1909; Princeton Architectural Press, 1994.

VAN DER RYN, SIM AND PETER CALTHORPE. *Sustainable Communities: A New Design Synthesis for Cities, Suburbs, and Towns*. Sierra Club Books, 1991.

VALLE, ERICK. *American Urban Typologies: Key West, Florida*. Village Publishers, 1995.

WEISS, MARC A. *The Rise of the Community Builders: The American Real Estate Industry and Urban Land Planning*. Columbia University Press, 1987.

WHYTE, WILLIAM H. *City: Rediscovering the Center*. Anchor Books, 1990.

WHYTE, WILLIAM H. *The Social Life of Small Urban Spaces*. Conservation Foundation, 1980.

WILLIS, CAROL. *Form Follows Finance: Skyscrapers and Skyline*. Princeton Architectural Press, 1995.

WOLFE, TOM. *From Bauhaus to Our House*. Farrar Straus Giroux, 1981.